Dedication/Acknowledgement

To, my best friend, constant companion,
my time traveling buddy, my love
and my inspiration, my wife, Eileen

Dennis John Ferado

Table of Contents

Table of Contents

Dennis John Ferado

Table of Contents

WE WERE YOUNG LOVERS

I found a light somewhere inside me
That keeps telling, telling me so
We were young lovers somewhere in Paris
You painted posters I painted poems

It was the end of the eighteen hundreds
I was your canvas you were my rose
You squeezed my hand when I first told you
You were the one who made me whole

You dressed in violet with ribbons and lilacs
You held my arm while I hummed a tune
Old women sold flowers the Seine filled with children
Artists sold paintings that long afternoon

While we had dinner soft shadows of sundown
Flowed through the window of a curtained saloon
We toasted our joy then swore on an oath
We'd always be lovers in life's spinning loom

You are the breath of the breeze by the ocean
Where ripe summer winds gently touch shore
I am the fire eternally burning
Searching you out forever more

You are the moon on the breast of the evening
when drapes of day begin to fall
I am the sun and the spark of the daybreak
you are the other half of my soul

"It matters not who you love, where you love, why you love, when you love or how you love, it matters only that you love." --John Lennon

"Love is not in the one who is loved
Love is in the one who loves."--Plato

LOVE IS IN THE ONE WHO LOVES

I can't see the air but I know that it's there
It fills my sails moves this vessel along
The best things in life are to love and to share
When we give of ourselves we surely grow strong

Just one thing I have to keep in my head
And remember what old Plato said:

"Love is not
In the one who is loved
Love is in the one who loves"

When the curtain falls and the dance has ended
And I find myself in another time and place
All the old deeds and misgivings upended
Dancing to a different tune with another face

Just one thing I have to keep in my head
And remember what old Plato said:

"Love is not
In the one who is loved
Love is in the one who loves"

BANISHED FLOWERS

I can't cram thunder in a box
Ride lightning till it's subdued
Fold a snowflake in half
Send the rain back upstairs
Hide the wind in my shoe

I can't pinch a ghost on the rump
Make pure gold out of base lead
Stuff a flood in a bowl
Stop you from growing old
Tear the years all to shreds

But with my weary homesick eyes
If you'll permit me I'll go
Nudge the thoughts in your skies
Fish the stream in your heart
Where banished flowers grow

L to R Dennis, Mom, little sister Margie & Dad

WE WILL SURVIVE

We trundle our barrel and bundle around the boulevard of life
Filled with joys, hopes, fears, dreams, sorrows and strife
Like ocean foam that kisses the shoreline's lip then disappears
Our loved ones are here to teach, love, wipe away fears
Then they are gone and we're set on our own path of duty
In the arms of a southerly breeze in the clutch of winter's beauty
From the bursting of spring to November's end of things
But as the bear sleeps and, like december's slumbering trees

We will survive

When you are weary, ruffled, been knocked to the ground and
The beauty of the bloom faded, the petals scattered around
When you are drunk on happiness or shattered by sadness
Remember the love you had that filled your heart with gladness
Tired from hope and fear the waves and gales of our earth
Cannot be stilled yet continue to give us priceless new birth
And we travel on with our one way ticket through time
In sightless peril drifting through the silent darkness of space
But like the sun in the morning we will continue to shine

We will survive

THE STRANGER

Once myself had met a stranger
swaddled in robes of gray mourning
in the bosom of the city
rambling through an ancient graveyard
painted with the hues of autumn
enshrouded in the morning fog.

Couldn't get any sleep last night
I only drowsed in bumpy dreams
savage thoughts like the pounding rain
vaporizing and cracking seams.

Brave heart of mine do not take flight
grievous thinking can make you slain.

Drifting through the purple fore-dawn
rippling skin in the morning air
dancing with the cordial south wind
till I spun and stumbled sideways
wrestling with the mighty north wind
till I was breathless, bruised and dazed.

I watched the grape grow plump with juice
and then I plucked it off the vine
vanishment I would introduce
true sorrow slaps the meanest blow
and leaves the thickest, scarlet welt
for all to see and all to know.

Continued...

Dennis John Ferado

Now that stranger in the bone-yard
coming at me like a phantom
spoke: "I'm weak and I am harmless
but leave the dead once they're entombed
vainly clinging ever feebly
to the walls of our mother's womb."

Silent as morning dew appears
his eyes went throbbing through my head
I turned and he had disappeared
fading star my silent witness
not consenting not protesting
winked down at me in ghostliness.

SWEET BREEZE OVER STRAWBERRY FIELDS
(missing John)

I feel slapdash and romantic
The interred spring has begun to rise
A balm for the bones
Lubricating the soul and
Lounging in the marrow
Diffusing mounting depression
Simmering essences
Of wishes and dreams
This wave could last forever
I can imagine all the people
And I can hear you singing
Strawberry Fields Forever

Me be slapdash and romantic
Inhaling scents of naked flowers
Delirium of love builds
Faith where there was none
Forcing the wolves to sleep
Liberating oblivion
Calming tense flayed nerves
Enrapturing the mind
Sweet breeze I will endeavor
And continue to imagine peace
And I can hear you singing
Strawberry Fields Forever

Dennis John Ferado

GRANDMA

Grandma was the only one
Who ever loved me free
There were no strings attached
To the love she gave to me
Grandma's eyes were big and wise
Her face was framed in gray
She would bounce me on her knee
Smile and then she'd say

Sonny boy with curly hair
Someday you'll be a man
Take this love i give to you
And spread it through the land
And don't go chasing rubies when
There's diamonds where you stand

Grandma's hands were soft and warm
To dust away my tears
When she held me in her arms
They'd wash away my fears
I would fetch her walking-stick
And we'd stroll down the street
She would take me by the hand
And say these words so sweet

Sonny boy with curly hair
Someday you'll be a man

Take this love i give to you
And spread it through the land
And don't go chasing rubies when
There's diamonds where you stand

Dennis & Grandma far right

My Grandma was Irish, her name was Catherine (Kitty) Kelly and she arrived in NYC in1902 when she was sixteen--all alone. She had that inbred Irish wisdom many of the Irish have and a wonderful way of communicating it. I remember her as if she were still with me. My memory of the many pearls of wisdom she told me, during the few years I had her, all came in short sentences. I've tried to gather them into a sort of poem to the best of my remembrance. I never found out what a ragamuffin was until long after Grandma was gone.

ADVICE FROM GRANDMA
(Ragamuffin)

Beware of those with their heads below their shoulders
watch out for the ones with them up in the clouds
mind those who flatter and disguise what they are
about, keep clear of all deplorable rogues of deception
you'll recognize them when they open their mouths
Trust no one and fear the worst that can happen
beware of lingering louts over your left shoulder
find the object of your flame of passion
hold on tight and continue to grow bolder

If you're a painter go after that masterpiece
a dancer? then tango across your map of life
or sing your song whatever it be, loud and clear
let it ring all the way to down-under from here.
When you've married sometime off in the future
and committed yourself to the one you'll call dear
your children shall be your grandest gifts from nature
They're yours for a moment keep them from fear
cherish their lives encourage and nurture

Try not to splinter when the thunder claps
banish your shyness don't cut with your
rage or get drowned in the tide of fanciful traps
but play your music and fill up your page

Some things are precious don't take them lightly
empathy and love are paramount for the soul
keep your heart open let it shine brightly
without these things the spirit will wither and fold
bestow of them freely beginning today
love is the most difficult to give away
if you do these things the most scrumptious
passions will all come rumbling and tumbling your
way and you will be fine my little ragamuffin

I WONDER:

At the mysteries of the universe,
I marvel at the infinite possibilities of the soul,
The endless tributaries and rivulets churning
In one lifetime and the choices we are tortured with;
I am bamboozled by the secrets in the animals eyes
Souls who yearn to speak, I am mystified by the
Miraculous trees their song is strong and moves my
Foundation; I am lightning struck, awed by acts of
Nature's unmatched fury and resistant forces; I am
Boggled by a living earth who gives us everything we
Need as we antagonize poison and torch it--yet it
Endures--I am amazed by every living thing and its
Individuality, the planets in their mathematical paths,
The sun who gives us life, the moon who moves the
Waters, the geometrical coordination of organic matter
As I walk past myself.

MOON-WHITE FACES

In the evening's rush of silence
Ravaging hands hurl you awake
You brush the darkness from your eyes
Wriggle off your ebony cape

Moon-white faces call to you

Fluttering bird break from your cage
Blow through the tubes of the city
Numberless eyes passing you by
Soul-searching eyes without pity

Moon-white faces white balloons

Fearless as a New York pigeon
Your heart refuses to take flight
Rain drumming down all around you
Wet moon-white faces in the night

Moon-white faces haunting you

BURNING RAGE

You don't know my life dear friend
Nor the roads of endless ends
The twisted trails I've traveled down
So many times I have been around
The queen of hearts I loved too hard
She took the deck and dealt the cards
The night I sat beside the dealer man
While she sat at his other hand
This fool stayed put with just 3 fours
And she walked out the open door
You see a time ago I did believe
A time would come I'd be relieved
But I was wrong and lost my faith
And wound up here behind this gate
A bitter man must eat his rage
Or chance a life inside the cage
Shiver out on a windy ledge
Spend my time on the razor's edge

She led the way where I was blind
She held a lamp up to my mind
Till she ran off with the dealer man
Way down south to the Yucatan I
Caught up with them in that hotel lobby
And shot him down like it was my hobby
Now she sits and stares without a will
Inside the house for the broken and ill

From my cell they can hear me wail
Wasting away in this Mexican jail
Late at nights I sing a weeping song
"The queen of hearts she did me wrong
I won't be free 'till a done old age for
I could not control my burning rage"

WRITTEN IN HER EYES

Saw her late one night on a southbound train
Said her life was filled with dark twisted lies
I did not even know the child's first name
But I knew--all, was written in her eyes

As they glittered, shone brightly with a hopeful glow
Her eyes still held the weight of misery and woe
Just like the sad eyes of a heartbroken work horse
Much too heavy for anyone to bear such force
A restless creature of the night, adrift below
Stuck amidst darkness, loneliness, shadows and fear.
Love is nil, thorns of agony come verging near
Pushing her straight backwards onto the ledge unseen
Not night, day, heaven, hell but a place in between
Delusion, confusion, and a region unknown
So many are lost there, where there's no place to lean
Where chunks of reality plod her mind and roam
A place where she could peer and see into her past
It's a district she would soon begin to call home

Vanishing Wind

*Storms gather in the bliss of solitude and in the sea
of imagination while the stress of want, the indignity
of need, the fragments of fantasies and the cinders
of careless love vegetate. We are the fires that
consume one another, the clubs that bludgeon and
the blades that slice. We wrestle in the currents of the
Hell Gate, off course, chewing memories, spitting them
out. Swallowing the rusted, pointed edges of the self
digesting them and growing ill. We are children of
Mondays speaking with the night-silence and tangoing
with the days. Soon to float in crumbled seclusion
spattered by the dried blood of yesterdays friendships
that drift farther and farther from the shoreline disappearing
into the horizon with their joys and their poetry stained
with sweat and urgency. The shards of miseries, fugitive
pieces of love, shavings of trust and the stones of
exasperation continue to reign with splinters of actual
seeing. With the loneliness of the moon in the soul we
walk shoeless in shadows mindless of direction as secret
as the dark mountain's haunting melodies we are dust and
mud, rain and flowers, sunshine and darkness; we are
vanishing wind.*

Time On Hand

"When people walk away from you, let them go. Your destiny is never tied to anyone who leaves you."--Marilyn Monroe

THE EYES OF NORMA JEAN

Not distant or remote but
With a touch of melancholy
As though in mourning
Are her eyes
Did she feel like November's
Last leaf on the tree
As she walked in shadows
Of peril and naked
Vulnerability
I see into her blues
The soul in the cage
In breathless mystery
Grief without malice or rage
After so many years
Eyes that continue to plead
Does anyone truly see me

THE SPELL OF THE CHASE

The moon's a full yoke that flies through the sky
The dew in my mind is starting to dry
The sweet scent of flowers perfumes my nose
With mars in the sky a hot ruby rose
Moon casting shadows of sad city trees
The spell of the chase is now upon me

Run through the streets to the sound of a bark
That rings in my head and stabs at my heart
Soft rolling thunder crescendoed and crashed
Webs of white lightning 'cross deep water flashed
Wild wailing winds start to whistle and rise
I scream at the vastness--black angry skies

An old dusty dream that somewhere went wrong
Musical box plays a memory song
Turned-up old picture an image of you
A pressed gardenia and friends that are few
Since you danced on my heart's yet to be free
The spell of the chase is down upon me

The spell of the chase is upon me
I am pulled by the currents of stream
The waters of change are demanding
And i feel like i'm lost in a dream
But i'm not and the tide keeps rising
So i'll run with the wind by my side
The footsteps of doubt far behind me
And the light of new life in my eyes

THE NIGHT GOES ON FOR DAYS

Askers takers fast money makers
Breakers fakers shortchange pocket-shakers
Sashay up beside you say they want to guide you
Through the misty maze follow me i'll hide you
In another place where the air is thick with haze
Where wild women and liquor flow
And the night goes on for days

Hawkers balkers freeloading paupers
Lodgers dodgers lawyers queens and robbers
Lost in a shore-less sea rumbling silence filling me
Rustling winds of time and a voice that said "you're free
On the doorstep of eternity you stand in a daze
But blind eyes can see so much more
Where the night goes on for days"

Batters shatter midnight mad hatters
Drinkers tinker with lonely eye winkers
Deceptive dreams devour chances by the hour
Shifting shadows shower the path to the tower
Moonlight through the ashen oak shows me other ways
Could it be the final hour
Where the night goes on for days

YOUR LOVE WOULD MAKE ME SING

I used to walk the city streets and try to find a meaning
To subway stares and women's wares faces go by dreaming
I ran the race of love and hate and scarcely felt a feeling
Yet through it all I still recall the touch that was so healing
I took a walk in the park today and that touch was on my mind
I seem to miss you most of all when autumn fills the sky
You could dance on the wing of a song you were everything
You'd pick me up when I went wrong then
Your love would make me sing

So I will take an airplane to a far off distant shore
Wild flying geese life's new lease strange faces at my door
Soon I'll feel warm-watered sands to the beat of a one-man band
Tiny towns foreign sounds I'll take chance by the hand
We moved together through parts unknown our love was like a dream
Now I hear your voice in morning's night like a distant tambourine
Restless nights of endless flight I'm running in a ring
As I go I think of the time when
Your love would make me sing

Oh your love would make me sing
For you I'd do most anything
Now I'm so lonely and I'm so blue
I can't live honey without you

EILEEN

January 31st. 1214. Claire, a special friend of mine. An amazing lady who has decided that this morning she will leave this earth because her pain is far too great to go on living. The doctors had come to her home at 9:30 and put her to rest. We had met on facebook, 5 months ago, after she had commented on my poetry, and quickly became close friends. We'd chat every morning for a couple hours when I awoke around 7:00 am. Belgium is 7 hours ahead of our time so it would be 2:00 pm for her. Because of the time difference she told me "I am older than you,"

Throughout the day I'd receive short messages from her which I would respond to. In the evenings, we'd talk again between 9 and 11:00 pm, my time, 4 and 5:00 am her time when her pain-filled day was just beginning. I learned about Claire's life and illness (cancer) and she learned about my life. Her breeding and my own were at extremes yet we became friends. Her suffering was extraordinary, she could not sleep, barely ate, and for the past 2 years only left her house to see a doctor. For you, sweet Claire:

LADY CLAIRE

Some eyes blemish the soul
Some eyes gleam with repose
Never met in person
But I know your eyes glowed

Your heart's been scraped from too much misery
Weighted down and tortured with wretched gloom
Despair swells, it wells up inside of you
Alone, all alone in your lonely room

Pain has colonized your mind and body
Said, you only needed someone who cared
So unescorted, there is nobody
No daughter to hold your hand or be there

"Life's too painful," is the only reason
You'll search for a place quieter than sleep
Where white roses bloom through every season
Where a river runs through a forrest deep
The scent of roses will fill days and nights
A place you can go and silently seek
Pure shades of majesty and sweet delights

This flickering candle once burned brightly
But the twinkle in your eye has vanished
no sleep time--you toss all around nightly
As they flock about, vultures all in sight
Soon it's over and you'll be over there
Rest peacefully, now, my sweet Lady Claire

IF MY WINGS COULD EMBRACE YOU

If my wings could embrace you
Starving children of the world
Universal boy and girl
Gentle old ones in turmoil
The lost and the souls confused
Who have drifted much too far
All the lonely at the bar
The wanderer without job

If my wings could embrace you
In your silent scream of night
Through the pain that brings you fright
In the shadows and in light
Over breathing strips of green
With golden emerald sheen
Through whisperings never seen
All dimensions in between

If my wings could embrace you
From the bed of your sorrow
To mountains of tomorrow
In this time we have borrowed
When the north wind starts blowing
Through the pangs of you going
Through the fires of growing
Knowing there's no other road

THE HAUNTING

Old woman walking alone
Along the east river's edge
Barefooted moving through
Moonlight in an off-shoulder
Cape stopping at the foot
Of the fifty-seven
Stone steps
I stood on the tower
Gazing down on this flower
And I watched her collapse
Stunned as her soul lifted
Glimmered and drifted then
Slithered up into the night
Floated close to my face
I reached out to touch
It vanished in flight
I let out a gasp looked
Back down the stone steps
The old lady was nowhere in sight

MEMORIES
(Run Frankie)

Fire-escapes and back yard weeds
Two for the money yet baby sleeps
Kick the can out in the street
Hurry Frankie and buy the meat
Run Frankie run if you can
Hurry Frankie here comes the man
You're gonna get it when pop gets home
You hit your sister now she won't come home
Hot potato in an empty lot
A cherry bomb will blow that lock
Stickball played on a crowded street
God that sweat felt so sweet
Johnny broke his arm yesterday
Mary lost a tooth
Patsy plants a seed today
Lets all pray
That it takes root

Growing up near a river becomes part of one's soul

I CAN HER THE RIVER WHEN SHE SINGS

Sky sounds like Chopin's Opus 53
Clouds rolling in a cleansing mode
Wind's gale tugging at my wings
Storm is rolling up the road
I sense the river when she wants to sing

Trees are chanting I hear their harmony
Leaves are shaking in multiple tones
My feet are swift like the crackling waters
The teeth of the night bite into my bones
I feel the river she's about to sing

I heed the wind the wind is very wise
I listen to trees they know many things
Sometimes they howl sometimes they sigh
I met a bird who taught me to fly
Now I can hear the river when she sings

East River photo by Thomas Pryor

THE CONDUCTOR

He is a dam through which all sounds enter
Wrapped in blue-evening's twinkling shawl
The river glides, sings a wordless tune
Something forgotten no longer recalled
The sublime voice of the universe howls
The river now sways in step with the moon
It cares for nothing keeps bad company
Trees voices take flight in a lyrical croon
The stars are aligned in brisk harmony
Rustling bushes rumble in low base notes
The grass sings tenor in their new green coats
The strains of this music weave savage like
The west wind humming sky flashing lightning
The cold cracked concrete path is now frightened
Bright rods of musical tones stun the night
O soulful tune conducted by Triton

CHILLY DAYS AND CHILLY NIGHTS

The autumnal air was invigorating
As I walked my dog through the park
The wood was dense and unlit
Trees shivered in spearing silver moonlight
Casting jumpy shadows then
I spied him on a bench alone in the dark
Staring fixedly out over the silent river
My eyes followed his eyes to their mark

A gauze of fog covered the water
As things began drifting by:
A faded batch of shattered promises
A bleary photograph of past intimacy
A hazy spill of recognition
A flash of ancient secrecy
A disappearing smile of old companionship
A dim pool of remembrance
A half recalled dream of significance
A vague patch of warming recollection

Stiff in sorrow rigid in remorse cemented in loneliness
Statue of stone i sat down beside the old man
He spoke to me through burnt-out eyes:

"This hungry heart is starved for love it yearns for
Someone to come and give it nourishment, to fill the
Empty spaces of a life, give meaning to
Chilly days, substance to these chilly nights"

DOWN TO THE RIVER

(i heard it through the walls
the neighbors next door
momma telling poppa)

"Ashamed to die as perplexed and dumbfounded as you are?
Befuddled as the day you came into this sad, sore world?
Mandolin dings, violin squeals, the big drum bangs slowly
Breezes of longing, rhythms of life sweep on over you
Voices of tortured spirits from distant fields call your name
Where dark is the wood, murky the path, comatose the souls
Poor souls standing in cloaks of mournful sophistication
That's where all the bread grows
stale with age and green-spotted mold
You dance, shuffle your shoulders in syncopation and hear
The hurtful lamentations of bruised, suffering women and
Feel the pain, fear, confusion of all the young innocents
Your shadow orbits you, a quickened dance of frustration
Bury all your troubles and woes for dead men sleep soundly
Take that hollow broken husk bear it down to the river"

BENEATH THIS SURFACE
(he)

He is a lion whose pride has vanished
Like dew embracing the morning flowers
Choking on the pangs of forgetfulness
A slab of concrete has replaced his heart
He was her bud-blooming protective tree
As she cuddled under the shade of he
Shameless lovers in their youth bound to go
Up the stairway of their eternity
Now, here, below the weight of sparkling snow
He hears the creaking of the leafless trees
Their moaning roots reach down gnarled and twisted
Frozen in earth by time and by degrees
And beneath this surface a river flows
Its echo rushes up and calls to he

SLEEP THE SLEEP
(surveying Hell Gate)

I muse into the mystic
Hypnotic river and discover
A taste of unknowable
Peace. Oh sweet
Debauchery of
Slothfulness take me
Away, dream me
away

Seduced by the city's coming
Night the breezes off the river
Embrace my soul, kiss
My face, breathe the
Soothing unknown into
My lungs and wrap
Me in their woeful mantelet

I lounge in stillness and stare as
My own shadow enters me
Peacefulness cover me, fill
Me up with something
Glorious, cast your
Spell and let me
Sleep the sleep of
Morpheus

ITS THAT KIND OF NIGHT

As I move through Broadway
The rain keeps falling down
People in a hurry shufflin' all around
Some in darkened hallways
With broken over-lights
Honey I'm so lonely
Its that kind of night

Its that kind of night moves something deep in me
Its that kind of night when thinking makes me be
Back in your arms again where living was so right
Honey I'm so lonely it's that kind of night

All night long visions of your flight
Darlin' I'm so lonely it's that kind of night

On that misty morning
I awoke and found you gone
Like a haunting song your spirit lingers on
Walking-dreams of you dear
In this moon's jaded light
Honey I'm so lonely
Its that kind of night

PARADISE NOCTURN

The heat and thickness of the day
Began to dissipate, dusk slithered
Down a flaming horizon, swirls and
Patches of purple and blue stained
A creamsicle sky announcing the rising
Full moon

Sniffing drifting odors
Carried on tropical winds as a
Renegade piece of something
Squirted across the
Heavens

Sounds of the approaching evening
Caressed and lulled: in the distance
A cawing concert of passing birds;
Nearby the persistent whooshing
Of waves on sand; boughs
Rose and fell with shifting breezes;
Creature sounds struck and rippled the
night like pebbles cast into
a motionless lake

MORNING WINE

She had a half-moon frown
Until the sun blew in through
The unclosed window
Spreading warm butter
Across her bed and
Opening her eyes.
A robin proffered
A snappy tune,
Sparrows played tag
In the jacaranda tree
Just beyond her window.
She smelled lilies on the bloom
And she became drunk on the
Morning's wine.

SCARLET and THE PREACHER

O Scarlet
The lamppost follows you
Buildings mutter to one another
Subway screeching like
A scalded alley cat
Rain slashing, sewers slurping.
Only you do you deceive
As grinding years besiege
Riding the dread of gloom;
You enter the room of moan
You see the gouging on the wall
Smoldering embers flicker and snap
Scattering ashes escape
Pensive musings are riven
A blinding storm of feelings
Rabbeting thoughts of confusion
Rattling through your brain
Leave a disrupting residue.
Moonlight dozes on the hardwood floor;
Scarlet, you sweep your brush
Through your vermilion hair
Sun Belt evangelical with sinister eyes
Bottomless chasm, inside lives an ill angel
Living on stolen desires and depraved lies
A soul that knows nothing other than betrayal.

He stares at you with menace
In his dirty eyes, smirk on lips
Furrows of foulness etched on his face
Dank of spirit, vacuous of heart
Bleak of eye, peppered with rage.
He moves towards you
Peering from the shadows
A clutch of chimeras leer, you are
Greeted by a flurry of mumbling.
Fed-up with harmful deeds and the iniquity
Lurking in the human heart
Chewed up by terminal wickedness
Threshed by angry winds from working mouths
Of imploding individuals. You are
Shaken by such brutality and it
Fills your heart with fallen snow
You pick up your bag, gaze down at
The preacher, you clean off your
Knife, and now, quickly, you must go

The only difference is that this is now done
legally through the in-justice system

HANGUMHI

They kicked in his door and dragged him from his
Wife and four children, blindfolded, they smuggled
Him away in silence, men in white hooded gowns
He heard whispers darting back and forth as they
Carried him into the woods the odor of hate ugly
And putrid soaked the air and drenched his nostrils
His body trembled, his mind quaked, his spirit
Crumbled before their eyes
Like love gone away freedom is never
Cherished until lost. Still, Mr. Smith, you sit and sigh
And gobble food. With your uninhabited heart
Alone without a cause, as the shouts
Continue to ring out Hangumhi
Hangumhi, Hangumhi

NOT QUITE RIGHT

The rhymester in his fine prime
Garbed in fierce agitation
As the poet walked behind
They plodded and they stumbled
Through the heat, rain and the smog
Seeking helpful elation

The mimic with rowdy brain
Searched chaos for solitude
Chose to walk through falling rain
Lived in the dark, strolled the park
Tried to out swim all the sharks
Wanted no part of falsehood

Arrows from tongues so well shot
Dipped in viper's vile venom
Causes blistering white hot
Sets fever makes believers
Of those who refuse to see
Drop down the chute to Bedlam

Moved away the rolling rock
Banshee rose up in his face
He saw the hands on the clock
Time melts, it up and flies by
Now he hears earth's final sigh
Joy has abandoned his space

The clown in his stark laughter
Dwelled in the dark lake of life
Sought truth in the hereafter
He'll go with the ocean's knell
Heads straight into the strong swell
Sharpened up his Bowie knife

The juggler juggles in vain
Stabbed by silence in moonlight
Built ramparts around his brain
Strikes out to set himself free
Another fine mystery
Makes all things seem not quite right

MY DADDY

When I was free with the ones
Who are still free from knowing
My daddy could run between
The gray ribbons of rain

And when I was down and
My sadness was showing
He'd say come on boy
Smile through the pain

As the wheel turned the years
And we grew a bit older
He could still walk between
The drops from the sky

He never got wet and with
One arm on my shoulder
He'd say "come under hear son
I'll keep you dry"

And his wings would embrace me
Soothe my screams in the night
When nightmares would chase me
All through my night's plight

When his time was upon him
With such power and pain
I stood there beside him
Angry saddened and drained

He said "come closer my boy"
And he mumbled my name
"Now give me your hand,
There is no one to fight with
There is no one to blame"

When my dad was passing, nearing the age of 72, during his final two days, he told me whenever he fell asleep he would find himself flying around the world. He didn't know how but he knew someone was with him. He saw his life as a youth and his entire family as they grew older. He said he saw all the suffering and the joy that was going on all over the earth. Tears rolled down his cheeks as he told me these things. This is for you dad.

I'M DREAMING
(for you Dad)

Sometimes I would rather be
floating now then drifting free
each new cloud caressing me
the wind blowing through my hair
my mind losing every care
when I go falling through the air
I'm dreaming
I see the shiny airplanes gently fly
while parachutes are floating from the sky
I was so young and strong back then
singing songs and proud back then
how the ladies loved me way back when
can't shake these thoughts from my mind
as delicate as the finest wine
I believe there's nothing left to find
I'm dreaming
I see the shiny airplanes gently fly
while parachutes are floating from the sky
Look at me falling free
screaming way down inside
I believe someday I'll see
but now let me hide in my mind

Christmas with dad, 1979: A couple of years after this photo was taken my dad passed away. The doctors had told us on March 25th that it would be impossible for him to make it through the day, much less the night. He could barely speak but we were still able to communicate with him right up to the end. We held his hands and sat with him the entire day. The doctors couldn't understand what was keeping him alive and Eileen and I were so confused we didn't know what day it was. But my father soon let us know why he waited to die, the following day, on March 26th.

NO ONE CALLS ME SWEETHEART ANYMORE
(Dad)

His bony hands on my
Two cheeks caused a
Numbness to rise in my spine
He gazed into my eyes with
His beautiful baby-blues
And they caressed my spirit
He pulled me closer with
A start
His chapped lips brushed my
Cheek with a soft kiss
His cracked and tired voice
Had a sudden surge of
Tender strength
He whispered
In my ear as his two hands
Haloed my face
"Happy birthday sweetheart"
The next day he was gone

I USED TO SWING WHERE
THE STARS ARE STRUNG
(man in dance hall singing and
doing the cha cha)

Because of lies a chunk of me has died but
I no longer reflect on suicide
Walking into the valley of unrest
Where gathering mounds of confusion crest
Do the dead really know when they've been wronged
By those yet living who will steal their songs

Now everyday is another chance but
Oh mama when I was young
How I could sing and I could dance
When I used to swing
Where the stars are strung

I scamper down into my cave of sleep
Bury my head and continue to weep
Dusty and rusty with darkness and gloom
I scuttle off into a private room
Emblems of hurt these tears fit like a glove
Dig a hole and bury these bones of love

Now everyday is another chance but
Oh mama when I was young
How I could sing and I could dance
When I used to swing
Where the stars are strung
When I used to swing
Where the stars are strung

SAD EYES

Our dreams are like ashes they blow in the breeze
We chase after quickly with one life to leave
I know you from somewhere your smile has no schemes
It sure wasn't heaven it must be my dreams
Perhaps a warm morning so golden and fine
Did I stumble to you all drunken and blind
Did you stretch out your arms to take me inside
Did you give me your love and then let me hide
The hard ways of this world are wicked and wise
And all of its sadness lies deep in your eyes
Did I come to you screaming out of the night
Did you quiet my crying make it all right
Ideas are like pictures that hang up to float
We watch them go by as they go up in smoke
Did I take it for granted your love to keep
When you wiped my brow and then rocked me to sleep
The tattered hand of winter smacks at my cheek
The wind-swept snow covers up my frozen feet
Will I see you again like birds from the south
Will I see your sad eyes or kiss your warm mouth

Sad eyes my mind keeps trying
Sad eyes my heart keeps dying

MOMMA'S RADIO

Momma's radio played Hank and Patsy
Big brother made me listen to Caruso
Little sister kept me in my running shoes
Being in between just made me whacky
Daddy learned me everything I know and
Momma taught me how to sing the blues

She had giving grace that she could unfold
A bigger heart would be hard to find
Her gift was to never grow old but
Mamma had weighty troubles on her mind

Some eyes become unwanted witnesses
Mamma saw something she shouldn't have seen
She swore that it was none of their business
But everyone knew she wanted to scream
It takes big money to run a holy place
So Mamma would walk to the corner bar
(that's when her hair began to gray)
She'd sit and stare at the entrance door
All grim and nasty sipping Tangeray
Leave when she couldn't stand it anymore
Come home at 3:00 am turn on the radio
And listen to that country music play

Momma's radio played Hank and Patsy
Big brother made me listen to Caruso
Little sister kept me in my running shoes
Being in between just made me whacky
Daddy learned me everything I know and
Momma taught me how to sing the blues

BY YOUR SIDE

When gray clouds come down
and rest their weight on your shoulders
When the moon's yellow yoke spills and stains the sky
When a weeping willow turns into a women and cries
That's when you know something's wrong
As the world goes spinning by
You think you are alone
But I'm right here by your side
By your side, by your side
I'm right here by your side
When you see that purple mansion
sink in a crimson-colored sea
When they say that things are
changing you say
they look the same to me
When you sit beneath that oak of
greatness and feel the sadness of a tree
That's when you know something's wrong
As the world goes spinning by
You think you are alone
But I'm right here by your side
By your side by your side
I'm right here by your side

NOTHING TO DO WITH ANYTHING

Some want more than what everyone has
And everyone wants more of everything
Still others want what no one else has
Me, I want nothing to do with anything

Some take more than what the takers take
And everyone seems to take everything
Still others take till you bend and break
But I want nothing to do with anything

I don't need a shovel when I'm standing in a hole
Don't give me any trouble when I'm knocked out cold
I can't use a double if it hasn't got my soul
Don't stroke me when my pony's just won everything
Leave me be I want nothing to do with anything

Everyone seems to want everything else
Many people want some diamond thing
No one ever seems to be themselves
So I'll take nothing to do with anything

Everyone keeps swerving into my lane
Eating tweeting texting some even sing
This whole place is completely insane
Just give me nothing to do with anything

I AM THE ONE

I am the rain that quenches your thirst
The poem that you studied and rehearsed
I am the hunger of the lost hound
I am the stones that hold you earthbound
I am the damp grass between your toes
I am the meadow where you run free
I am the echo in a grand hall
I am the singing bells when they toll
I am the oak of great dignity
I am the leaf that withers and falls
I am the One
I was the mountain where you now stand
Now I'm that rock beaten into sand
I am the tree with whom you ponder
I am that eagle with whom you fly
I am the friend with whom you wander
I am the dew that clings to your lips
I am the snake that crawls in the pits
I am the dust that gusts in your eyes
I am sensations hidden inside
Think you feel somebody by your side
I am the One
I am the strings in your rhapsody
I am the sea that streams through your veins
I am the root of your melody
I am the doorway into your mind
I am candles that gleam in your eyes
I am the twilight forever young
I am the song that cleaves to your tongue
I am the wind that lashes your face
Steals your breath lifts up that dress of lace
I am the space where the stars are strung
I am the One

Continued...

I am the walk you take in the sky
I am the cloud you rest on to sigh
The crack of the daybreak when you wake
Obsidian black seen when you sleep
I am the sheen that lives in your hair
I am the breezes you hear that speak
I am the blush that colors your cheeks
I am the branches starting to creak
When the trees are all frozen and bare
When you think that you sense someone there
I am the One

AND ON, AND ON, AND ON....

imploding individuals--excruciating evidence
fatalistic curiosity--sacrilegious defiance
diverse characterizations--tangible depositions
rejected imperfections--discontented practitioners
revolving psycho maniacs--obnoxious obstetricians
terminating undertakers--emotional instability
physical intimidation--industrial combustibles
heart breaking testimonials--coordinated catastrophes
congested imaginations--extenuating circumstances
exploding penitentiaries--unscrupulous clergymen
schizophrenic psychologists--paranoid psychiatrists
dejected educationalists--devastating contradictions
inflated pretentiousness--dishonorable politicians
supernatural revelations--medicated personalities
rejected interventions--neglected imperfections
indisputable limitations--irreversible frustrations
hesitating dispositions--melancholy resignations
justifiable aspersions--undeniable delusions
confusing philosophies--redundant complacency
inevitable remorsefulness--inhospitable transportation
cantankerous offhandedness--falsified investigations
"historical imperative"--"manifested destiny"
unconstitutional consistencies--Machiavellian attorneys
insidious manifestations--intensified gullibility
super subtle perceptibility--unappeasable anxiety
religious antagonism--hypocritical convictions
manipulating pedestrians--antagonizing aggravations
significant discourteousness--magnificent deceptiveness
consistent contradictions--persistent derogation
immeasurable insolence--undefinable unreliability
idiotic susceptibility--overabundant irrationality
irrevocable decisions--exceptional stupidity
unparalleled preconceived prejudice
and on and on and on....

TAR BEACH

Some of us get up and run
Off the streets into the sun while
Far below the pavements pound
The melting-pot keeps spinning 'round
When fire surrounds me and there is no escape
Its the top of the world via the old fire-escape
Solitude at tar beach I know I can find
In the heart of the city King Solomon's mine

No sand no water not a seagull to squawk
Just some pigeons that coo
And a sparrow that talks

From where I perch I see rivers' bend
The New York City Rockies that never quite end
My roof is a rose with whom I'm alone
And know in my heart I've never left home
Some of us get up and run
Off the streets into the sun while
Far below the pavements pound
The melting-pot keeps spinning 'round

GO TO THE ZOO

You slide through the night like a cat in the dark
You get to the corner jump into the stream
You swim and you sing you are a meadowlark
The water is good and humanity flows
You have nothing to do and nowhere to go
So you talk to people that nobody knows
You seek locations where the banished are led
You inhabit places no living soul goes
Some say you're crazy simply out of your head
They say you hear voices that no one can hear
You sulk in spaces where the living are dead
Get lost in the regions where turbulence grows
Some say that you are in it up to your neck
You go to the zoo break the lock on each cage

You're happy yet sad with your passion to wreck
Indulging in madness entangled in rage

MEAN JOSEPHINE AND BENNY THE BUM

She sang when she drank and had long golden locks
when ends didn't meet she'd shape-up at the docks
a hustler, a buster full of vim and vigor
quick on the temper with a hair-trigger finger
She was short and round and very heavy
she was a thief and drove a stolen chevy
Josephine Josephine mean Josephine

He was a gin-sock, grubby, a useless bore
most every night the face on the barroom floor
he was thin, silent and long with an ugly stare
he had beady gray eyes that looked into nowhere
He was abused, booed and used as a broom
he made people angry when he entered a room
Benny oh Benny poor Benny the bum

He was knocked off his stool by a smaller man
when she screeched to a halt in her red-hot new van
he climbed back on his seat with his head still ajar
as she barreled cross the room, bellied-up to the bar
She spoke "Hank, leave the bottle" it came out like a
scream
Hank moaned "Please no trouble mean mean Josephine"
Josephine Josephine mean Josephine

When their eyes met it was sheer heaven on earth
inside Josephine took place a new birth
she trembled like Jell-O with cold bumps on her spine
Benny's knees shook and knocked couldn't utter a line
The quiet kept mounting soon devoured the roar
quickly, she head-locked the bum marched out the door
Benny oh Benny poor Benny the bum

Stepping outside she said "Your about forty.
I'm twenty-nine and my friends call me shorty"
she tossed Benny into the back of her van
with a TV set and her other contraband
Shouting as she burnt rubber "I can spin on a dime
I stole me a bum, now Benny, you are mine"
Josephine Josephine and Benny the Bum

WITHOUT A FRIEND

Friendship is a gift from above,
Something to cherish pieces of love.
Down the hill and then around the bend,
Three leaves spinning in the swirling wind.
Sincerity is a true virtue
Nearly futile to discover
Rare, yet it's there.

Without a friend to call by name,
A body will sometimes quit the game.
In the landscape of the drifting soul
We cannot, will not, ever grow old.
Listen to the one who has no
One to listen to their story
But only you.

Without a friend I am a lock
Without a key, I stumble through life's
Symphony, a something that will not
Grow, roots without a tree, a stranger
Nobody knows, drifting around,
Without a home. Another thorn
Without a rose.

This was written on Memorial Day for all the men and women who have served and are serving

AMERICA'S CHILDREN - Precious, Unsung

You are the sons who've died too young
The husbands of wives whose lives came undone
You are the hearts that were taken away
From lovers and friends who grieve on this day
America's children precious, unsung

You are the fathers your children won't know
You are the children we'll never see grow
You are the sisters who healed and caressed
Brothers who helped us to grow and to dress
America's children precious, unsung

You are the children snatched from the hearts
Of parents who loved you right from the start
You are the ones the soldiers so bold
The lost pieces of millions of souls
America's children precious, unsung

WAY DOWN UNDER
(time was)

Walking all alone
Feeling like a sigh
Stretched out above is the
Sinful liberty of a clear blue sky
But you can see beyond
The planets and the stars
You have danced with venus
Ran and schemed with mars
Listened to the song of pain
From neptune's heavy rains
Way down,
Way down under

You have heard the rumbling
Tumbling voice of jupiter
Pounding in your brain
Like Niagara's rolling thunder
His sound is the same
But pluto was the one
Who tore your soul asunder
The thought of him still rankles
Who clung rudely to your ankles
Then pulled you way down under
Way down, way down
Way down under

STREET CORNER BUMS

Street corner bums and dancing clowns
Live where the moon makes the rivers go 'round
Madison avenue smarts with sandpaper hearts
Policeman drive taxis immigrants push carts
You've got to speak another language
Besides the one you do
Slang, jargon, park avenue
Any one will do

Two drunken sailors a worldly lap dancer
Move to the music of a hot cuban band
A dozen roses for the lady on the stage
But when she's home alone she turns another page
While the beer-drinking jester
Keeps on holding court
The princess and the pauper
Go prancing to the port

Starry-eyed virgins turn into street urchins
Hooker 'round the corner is in church with her daughter
Me I'm a joker working and getting older
While the tax man picks my pocket
And the landlord's rent sky rockets
But I'm gonna get over this feeling
That's getting me down

For all the taxi drivers in New York City
NEW YORK CITY SONG

Tight rope walkers, city stalkers
Come to meet you come to greet you
With the morning sun days begun
In New York City
Skinny ladies, hairline crazies
Push and shove as they live and love
In downtown's zone, right off Great Jones
In New York City

Heat so hot around mid-July
Chill so cold from a wintry sky
Spring and fall sheer beauty behold
In New York City
Buildings high dance with rolling skies
Sing with sadness, ring with gladness
It's evening time I'm feeling fine
In New York City

Taxi drivers, thieves and liars,
Beggars sinners, would-be winners
Creeps and clowns all hanging around
In New York City
Big time boppers, city hoppers
Wealthy women chauffeur driven
Run around in a rich man's town
In New York City
Through many days of wind and rain
I'm different now I'm not the same
Get so tired of ties that bind
I'm the one always running blind
From head to toe my name's not mine
In New York City

YOU AND I

Those bottle caps we used to save
And stick them on our shirts that way
And water guns we'd fill with ink
You can squirt but you cannot drink

You and I we've gone our own ways
Two trains moving east and west but
You and I have seen some good days

See two features on Saturday
Sixteen cartoons a place to play
Water balloon from off the roof
Might catch you in your Sunday suit

You and I we've gone our own ways
Two birds flying north and south yet
You and I have shared some grand days

Climb a mountain down in the park
Be sure you're home before it's dark
Drink a soda in shady haze
Trade Mickey for a Willy Mays

You and I we've gone our own ways
Travelers time has overlooked still
You and I have had some fine days

FRAGILE

Unreasonable love peering
Into my shadow side
Standing where the path forks
A famished tiger mewls
Inside my aching head
I spin in dizzying circles
And lose command of myself
Become dismal-minded

Organized things begin
Fragmenting, evenings go by in
Busted sighs as absence howls
In the night. This gobbet of
Perplexity weighs heavily
As I search for the unexplainable
Anxious inquisitiveness fills my mind
How precious, how fragile my friend

WHEN THE LAND IS BURNT DRY

If living was singing your voice has been sweet
While visions of medusa dance at my feet
If trying was flying you've flown for some miles
So stretch out your legs honey and rest for awhile

You've been there to comfort to hold and to soothe
You've got your own pain, I know that you do
I'm trying so hard I used to be strong
You sit and listen to my broken song

Without your love baby, without you along
I'd be so twisted up, I'd live all alone
By the river of madness in the valley of tears
With an acre of sadness on this planet of fears

You're a cool wind in august
A bird in the sky
You're rain from the clouds
When the land is burnt dry

I LET LOVE SWEEP ME AWAY

Now the nights are getting short
And the days grow long again
See the flower break the ground
I know winter's seen its end
This boy's heart beats fast today
I let love sweep me away

With the sun in Aries' sign
Feel the trembling of the earth
As the city shakes alive
And the streets fill up with birth
With the spirit of spring today
I let love sweep me away

The day force waxing stronger
The night force waning down
Its the time of the living
happy faces all around

I'm a joker and a fool
I have broken all the rules
Eternally young
I'm a rough one and a jewel
But since I met you today
I let love sweep me away

WE ALL BELONG TO EACH OTHER
(we are all one)

We all belong to each other we are all one
All through time we are the moon the stars and the sun
When young we are filled with love and with dreams
Then we grow up start building war machines
Given a sense of compassion now where has it gone
We hunt we kill we maim drive each other insane
And do our children most grievous harm and
Continue to ignore the oncoming storm but
We all belong to each other we are all one
All through time we are the moon the stars and the sun

We all have something to hide everyone is not all good
We all still die even when we do what we should
I knew a little boy who grew into a strong young man
Went off to a war to die in a strange foreign land
Someone stood there but I could not see a face
The form remained before me then I heard a voice
"Give ear and listen, it's humanity's final race"
This world is getting smaller things keep getting worse but
We all belong to each other we are all one
All through time we are the moon the stars and the sun

THEY CALLED MOM, MAGGIE

Way back in nineteen-twenty-six
Maggie had just turned twelve
Anna was seven, little Nora was six
They came home from school that day
Found grandpa George hitting my grandma
Nora was scared and began to pray
All morning George had been down at the bar
Maggie grabbed George Junior's baseball bat
She gave her mean poppa a real fine whack
He ran on down to the doctor's office
He had sixteen stitches when he got back
Oh, Grandma how'd you ever endure
And become the sweet angel I adored

Grandma & Grandpa, Nora, Maggie & Anna

Spend Your Nights With Mama
(remembering Janis)

In the morning babe
After you have gone
Everything I do love
Twists and bends all wrong
Then about noon time
I get all sick inside
Wondering to myself
Will you be home tonight
You gotta spend your nights with mama honey
You gotta share with me your pain
You gotta spend your nights with mama baby
While on this traveling train

It's the early evening
And I'm so all alone
Bourbon just won't do it
Darlin' please come home
Here's the other side of midnight
About a quarter to three
Rain is pouring down outside
And your not here with me
You ought'a spend your nights with mama honey
You ought'a share with me your pain
You ought'a spend your nights with mama baby
Before she goes insane

You said I wouldn't do it
But I can't take it anymore
This is the last time now
Watch me walking out that door
I know you hurt too babe
But your spirit I can't save
You're the captain of your own ship
And your boats on stormy waves
You should'a spent your nights with mama honey
You should'a shared with me your pain
You should'a spent your nights with mama papa
We could'a made it through the rain

LIFE IS TOO PRECIOUS

Blinded they stare while the gale has begun to blow
Its twisted, hidden, deep down inside in the dark
I know that we're here to love and to grow
So I vacate my head and inhabit my heart
Don't say a word when things start to show
Life is to cherish I know
Life is too precious to go

I plead and I hope and continue to try
Freedom begins with wanting to know
Open your ears unfasten your eyes
Beware of the fox it's just a disguise
Life is to cherish I know
Life is too precious to go

Like a reed in the wind I will weaken and bend
To the sound of sweet music when it comes to its end
I have studied and learned from the sky
For a thing to be born then something must die
These are the times men's souls need to mend
Yes life is to cherish I know
And life is too precious to go

AS I THINK
(why the children)

As I sit by my window and quietly listen
To summer's final pant of submission
I feel the crisp air of autumn seep into my pores
I think of days gone by of love and hate
Peace and war, brother, sister and much more

I think of real love so rarely found
Homeless souls scattered all around
I think of many things this night
Little ones and their wretched plight
And I think
Why the children of the earth
Why must they grow in all this dirt

As I sit by my window silently waiting for sleep
My mind's in a whirl it just cannot keep
An idea for too long a thought at its peak
With the moon in my eyes the cold on my feet
Think I'll lie back down try to get some sleep but

I think of love as sweet honey bits
Then I see burning bodies in a ditch
I think of many things this night
Friend and foe, black and white
And I think
Why the children of the earth
Why must they grow in all this dirt

Tomorrow we'll all wake to the same old pain and know
Nothing was accomplished except that it rained

DIRTY HANDS AND DUSTY JEANS

Rocks in my pocket holes in my shoes
Strings on my guitar have all been overused
Raindrops on my shoulders smile inside an eye
Chasing down a rainbow I'll tale a train to ride

Through the back roads of my memory
I can touch her face so tenderly
There, love lingers silently
There, minds drift in harmony

Daydream is one step beyond an empty fifth of gin
Call long distance three a. m. from Lazy Mary's Inn
Hand and hand to paradise a million miles from here
A thousand burning bridges we walked them without fear

No chains upon the ankles of a man who won't be loved
No teary eyes or broken dreams when time arrives to shove
A train leaves here tomorrow for dancing New Orleans
I know I'll be on it dirty hands and dusty jeans

THE ONLY NON-ILLUSION

I had a friend when he was young was no pilgrim to pain
He stood all alone a weed shadowed by flowers
He skidded through corridors built of slow motion
And danced with the beast of loneliness after hours

Insulted and tormented by a face from the past
Touched by a hand from another dimension
Rolled down the river of bourbon and rocks
Said he, there ARE ghosts, there is no contention

Lost in a garden where each plant--bloom and root
Created a different dream world than the last
He's slept in hallways, basements, on a snowy rooftop
It ended in confusion and mayhem but that's all past

He longed to plant a gentle kiss on the lips of death
He'd accumulated too many cuts and contusions
He died but he arose and bounced right back
Discovered love is all and the only non-illusion

Dennis John Ferado

I CAN'T STOP THINKING ABOUT THE PAST

I'm standing in a useless old boat
Can't catch a wind, fix a broken mast
Dressing up old words in a new cloak
This revolving shroud of night can't last
Things will look better in the morning
I can't stop thinking about the past
The sun bubbles up and makes his start
The sharpest blade will lose its edge fast
Searching for the language of the heart
The sweet nectar in my drinking glass
I can sooner walk away from me
I can't stop thinking about the past
Reading verse softened and contented
Looking back those days were rainbow cast
Youthful garment I only borrowed
Smiles I tried to keep within my grasp
Standing in the eye of tomorrow
I can't stop thinking about the past
I've never heard a giraffe complain
So I guess I haven't heard it all
They can't say my heart was ever feign
Time scoots by first your first then your last
Many souls gone yet not forgotten
I can't stop thinking about the past
I can't retrieve my vanishing thoughts
Like marbles bouncing down long stone steps
I love the sun when I'm overwrought
But moonshine stands me up makes me prance
Autumn colors vanish in a flash
I can't stop thinking about the past

L to R Dennis. brother George, sister Margie

THE NIGHT BELONGS TO PARIS

Mysteries everywhere Left Bank near the Follies Bergere
More than strangers with a shared past at the Hotel Monte
In Monmarte now seems to me flawless and matchless--and
The night belongs to Paris

Bound in bonds, touched by magic
shake your fragrance over me
Alive in your abundance I bite this rare fruit of dignity
Sights and wonders to behold, astound, enchant, enfold--O
The night belongs to Paris

Strolling through the Latin Quarter
Right Bank along the Seine
Down the Boulevard Saint-Michel
Staying at the Claude Bernard
Staring through the windowpane

Quiet early Sunday morning
This laundrette's wooden bench is hard
I watch the ladies sweep their sidewalks
In the tinkling rain
Night remembers everything and
Your mornings leave me breathless--but
The night belongs to Paris

The night knows things the new day has forgotten
When stars come out I'm another of your
wide-eyed paramours
Who flourish in your finesse--yes
The night belongs to Paris

When evening fades and the sun comes peeping over
rooftops
Find me nestled in the lap of your morning
Come the dusk you transmute
a gleaming diamond necklace--oh yes
The night belongs to Paris

THIS MOMENTARY TOUCH

You hear the sound of print less footsteps by the sea
The path of your departure is no longer free
The breeze, to you, whispers silent whirlwind passions
You trip backward over driftwood in fear's fashion

Nature's howling accents are filling up the night
What's baying at the moon is striking you with fright
Pulses pause teardrops burn your tender shallow cheeks
Are you awake or did you now get up to sleep

Your moves must be like the mystic liquid ocean
That stirs this wild earth and gives it living motion
Your eyes, I feel, are wells that go beyond the deep
They haunt me through the spring and autumn of my sleep

Good luck, I know, don't make the daystar spin and dance
Nor do great river currents ebb and flow by chance
I'm a rock in this raging river you may clutch
I'm your love-giver for this momentary touch

LET IN THE LIGHT OF LOVE
(thoughts of William Butler Yeats)

The rowdy spirit of youth swept on over you
Like a winter storm wind out at sea
Whisking away all withered leaves and weeds
Wandering plundering through the wasteland
Stumbling blundering through the dreamland
Poet faker minstrel in a restless land

Floating in limbo on the portal of trance
Slipping sliding doing the jumpy dance
Visions of youth laughter and sorrow
Through the fiery doorway onto the plains of chance
Bless the human kindness that was there to borrow
You're here today now make it through this dance

Break the chains that hold you down
On the wings of love get star-ward bound
Take the power from above
Hear and feel the rushing sound
And let in the light of love

As the mist ascended you thought you spied the dancer
Through the thickened woods that rustle windy answers
Among the many colored leaves of laughter
Who is this riddle reader who writes with every chance
A quizzical soft walker through modern times again
But can you know the dancer from the dance

OLD MAN IN DOORWAY

The night was stark and wintry
Only the bold roamed the streets
But sitting in the shadows
A broken man with bandaged feet.
Sifting through the ashes of all the time that he has
burnt.
Staring at the only picture of the ones that he has hurt.
He looked at me and said:

"Come here boy
And help this old man to his feet
Instead of thinking he will melt.
Why I've been through brothels and bar rooms and
Made my way from dark of night to bright of day,
Sung my songs both lusty and gay.
Probed the shadows of each stranger's twisted eyes
Searching for some structured disguise;
Down dark dank streets with my beams half open,
Past alleys all weary and broken,
While swimming in an ocean touched only by glass,
I watched the dream from the liquor fade into a mist
Then segue into the past."

Can't get Mrs. Martin and Mrs. Davis off my mind

TWO MOTHERS

In the silent night you hear a song
Drifting between heartache and despair
The piercing voice of a crying horn
This broken melody can't be repaired

You're troubled in mind, troubled in soul
Something that can never be reclaimed
Your little boy will never grow old
During the night you call out his name

Loneliness plants seeds of desolation
As old dreams come back to haunt you
Cultivating buds of stagnation
Turning into many shades of blue

This planet, a world of sheer madness
Snatched pieces of time float through your mind
Torment the companion of sadness
There's such dignity in your pained eyes

You sit to eat there's an empty chair
Barbed bramble and hurtful prickly vines
You can't comprehend why no one's there
As icy fingers claw at your mind

For you dear mothers I have one craving
Untroubled sleep and merciful waking

SAM AND THE BONELESS MAN

They walked in the place he had a smile on his face
Dressed kind of chummy with his redheaded honey
Strolling 'cross the room in loose harmony
Holding his arm she had a lock on charm
His hair was slicked back all shiny blue/black and
They sat at the table by the potted palm
They got up to dance and she tossed her head back
He was a boneless man moved like a rubber band
Across the dance floor their steps were true and sure
I heard him call her Sam she said, oh mi amore
As she danced and she danced with the boneless man

He said you can dance among the seven skies
Since seeing is tied to more than the eyes
You can balance on a tightrope that's who you are
I am just a prancer you are the star
Wise man knows when to step and when to glide
Come on Samantha lets put the world in a jar
Love is all we need to fly to the sky
He was a boneless man moved like a rubber band
Across the dance floor their steps were true and sure
I heard him call her Sam she said, oh mi amore
As she danced and she danced with the boneless man

Melodies filled her soul the moment of her birth
Now the music of her spirit keeps her on the run
She was Sadie Thompson she was Rita Hayworth
Beneath the turning ceiling fans they spun
Anything but loud there was a stunned hushed span
Everybody stared red dress flying everywhere
Tripping the light fantastic with the boneless man
He was a boneless man moved like a rubber band
Across the dance floor their steps were true and sure
I heard him call her Sam she said, oh mi amore
As she danced and she danced with the boneless man

Jimmy & Mary Patton's "perfect baby girl" and my very special godchild, Jessica Patton Suomala. Born in 1972, I wrote this later on for her 2nd birthday in 1974.

HAPPY BIRTHDAY JESSICA
(1974)

You blew into our hearts like a warm gentle breeze
Changing all our lives with your charms of expertise
The poetry of your nearness paints us with pride
In bleakness and sunshine slaves of your haunting eyes
Now we shove each other around, undignified
Who is going to hold you who will be satisfied
"Will someone take the baby while I go outside?"
Three of us scramble across the living room floor
Give her here, I'll take her. No! you had her before
Mental eyes that hypnotize what a grand surprise
Daddy toiled the earth and got nothing from its womb
But Mom lent a hand and now the sweetest rose blooms

Your gentle soul's sly little smile is enchanted
May the seeds of pain and outrage never get planted
May you drift far and easy but never get lost
And the lengthy map of years never show its course

BEHIND A WEATHERED BROW
(Pappy)

Pappy peddles papers down by the docks
Cold winds blow 'round his ears and through his socks
Pappy don't care too much 'bout tomorrow
Broken dreams, memories he'll never borrow
He's got them tucked behind a weathered brow
Cannily tucked behind a weathered brow

Fifty years before two thousand and ten
Young Pappy took the hand of sweet Megan
Just one year today since she's gone away
Trees turn green, summer's here, she's gone away
And he can't seem to keep her off his mind
She's safely tucked behind a weathered brow

Joseph was his baby only yesterday
Until war stamped a claim on his destiny
Now Pappy cries at nights for his only son
While Joseph drinks water from a broken gun
Pappy suffers on the streets at night

Sometimes Pappy dreams about his mama
An open door and through it comes his papa
No Pappy don't care too much 'bout tomorrow
Broken dreams, memories he'll never borrow
He's got them tucked behind a weathered brow
Fondly tucked behind a weathered brow

IN THE AMERICAN DREAM
(runaway's note)

"Confusion surrounds me in this atmosphere
I attempt to untangle fill up with fear
If I can't get my life high up on the hill
Well i think I might bend to some other will"

"Drug dealers all over they won't go away
They've got all the playgrounds there's no place to play
Children are murdered and you can hear them scream
Used and beaten in the American dream"

"Visions of doubt and shadowy fears
Shoot through my mind on an ache and a tear
Mamma's back home drinking in bed
Daddy's long gone he took drugs instead"

"America's children are in a real bind
Raped and abused then given drugs for the mind
They say 'follow a rainbow through fields of green
There're no nightmares in the American dream"

Some years back, Eileen and myself, along with her sister Sheila and Alejandro, took a weekend car trip to Boston. Eileen was our navigator and this is how things had gone.

THAT ROLLING BAY CITY PLACE

We were moving up the thruway in a rumble-seat car, Sheila, bouncing all around Alejandro puffed a big cigar. When the navigator said "you know I do not lie, if I don't get some lox and bagel with cream cheese on the side, I'll make you all so miserable that you'll begin to cry and then I'll get so physical you'll wish that you could hide." Now I'm a fool but not that big so we stopped for some fuel. Said, Sheila, with a smirk that I was self-tortured and cruel putting creole on my scrambled eggs was not very cool and she was right for later that night I looked like a jadrool.

We pulled up to Howard Johnson's where someone just broke in "they unlocked the locks now we have double locks" said the girl without a chin. Stuck in traffic as the rains came alongside the market place around and around nowhere to be found a little parking space. We drifted into the Government Inn and found a rumble-seat resting place. "Damn the rain" was Sheila's refrain as she ran with a frown on her face. Said, Sheila: "Why did you buy suspenders here by Boston Bay? said I "they hold my pants up I guess I'm strange that way." Bloody marys and pina coladas picked us up from feeling low, Alejandro winked through a cloud of smoke and said, "You see I told you so!

Now let me tell you something else" spoke Alejandro's lips "Keep your hands upon the table I'll take the bill and tips."

When, Sheila, said "let us find the freedom trail and march to Paul Reveres staring at the map I said "Through the maze and over here." We walked a ways beneath the navigator's stern and icy stare when she said "It's not there it's over here as she found us Paul Reveres. I asked a large man with a big mean face "Where is the oldest church?" "Follow the little red road" said he "but watch out for the lurkers who lurch, they'll take your clothes, your money, your car and you know you won't be the first. But you understand you're from New York and there I hear it's much worse." Well, we shuffled around through crooked Roman streets till we came upon this little man who sold clips to hold your sheets in place so you shouldn't ever have to make your bed any more and in the morning you can dash right out your door. Then where the gate front frescos fill the Sunday air, I could smell the closed Italian bakeries through the frescos stare. Columbus Day breakfast where girls outside the glass window raced while inside with sneakers "1" served "100" as sweat flew from her face. While echoes of Emerson blanketed that rolling bay city place.

L to R--Dennis, Eileen, Sheila, Alejandro

I had written four pieces after the collapse of the towers, which we had watched from our windows. This is one of them.

A HUNDRED TRAINS COMING

Fifty-two: I wish I could reach my wife. Who's going to take care of the kids if I don't make it down? I've got to get out. I've got to. I have to get to my family. They need me! We're moving so slow I wonder how long it will take? How long has it taken us to get this far? I don't know. Fifty-one: Everyone is so quiet. So orderly. I'll try her again. Maybe I'll get through, this time. I hope she's not out shopping at the market. Fifty: It's getting awful warm. Damn! Don't drop the cell phone. Stupid! I almost dropped my cell phone! That's all I need. I'll try again. Forty-nine: It's ringing! Come on Honey. Pick up. Where are you?

I never realized how much time elapses before the second ring begins--it's a small eternity. Nooo! The line went dead. The stinking line went dead. Forty-eight: At least we don't have to go up. It's a lot easier going down....that's not funny idiot. I wish we could move faster.... That woman who screamed. Forty-seven: What did she shout. "A large plane filled with people crashed into the building." Those people in the plane. Did they know they were going to die just before they hit? could they see it coming beforehand? The pilot! Forty-six: He had to see it coming. Damn! How could he hit this building? It's a beautiful day and you can see for miles. What the hell happened? Forty-five: I smell smoke. I don't know if I'm going to get out of here. Will any of us get out of here? I promised to take the kids to Disney World this year. Forty-four: They're going to hate me if I don't come home again. They won't understand until they're much older. No. Their mother will make them understand. Honey, I'm sorry. I'll try her again. Thank God for cell phones. Please, let me reach her.... I can't get through. It's still dead. If I could hear her voice... Forty-three: If I could say goodbye. I'd feel much better. I can't believe that no one is panicking. It's eerily calm in this stairwell.

Forty-two: I have four hundred and forty dollars in a coffee can down in the basement. With all the other coffee cans. They hold every nail and screw that I own. There's so many things around the house that have to be fixed. Forty-one: She'll never find that money. She could really use it now, if I don't get out of here. My "Sweet-baby" girl starts Kindergarten this year. Forgive me, my darling. What's wrong with this phone? Why can't I get through? Forty: Other people are getting through. Oh, that woman sitting in the corner crying. I'll talk to her. No! I can't. She's saying goodbye to someone. Someone she loves. She's saying goodbye? How does she know? I guess I know, too.

Thirty-nine: I wanted to get my "big-boy" his first two-wheeler this Christmas. This smoke is getting to me. Starting to burn my eyes. Who's that coming up the stairs? A firefighter. Thirty-eight: Here comes another one, and another. What are they crazy? They can't go up there. They'll all die. Here comes another one. He's looking right at me. He...he's just a kid...., and he knows. It's in his eyes--he knows and he keeps on walking up. What's that noise? That roaring, its deafening. Oh my God! it sounds like a hundred trains coming....

WOOD

He was a wild and sorrowful dirge
Played on a weeping violin
With a voice as soft as
The rustling of tumbling leaves
He was weary and timeworn
As an ancient redwood
And carried the grief
Of a burnt out forest
He was battered and spine-bent
As a hurricane-palm
And lonely
As a piece of driftwood
I watched him disappear through the trees
In a spluttering of sun and shadow

SOUL OF A PAINTER

The painter's soul lives in his brush
The poet's soul is in his pen
The cello plays a tragic note
Dancing treetops begin to blush

Littered moonlight acrawl on grass
Now see it all with restless eyes
And hear it all with keen-edged ears
Watching vague shadows skip and dash

Rest me down beneath the far stars
Guzzle star-shine on humpback hill
Fiddle and cello laced in song
Inside this canvas of Renoir's

SWEET STREET ROSE

Sweet Street Rose there my memory goes
To a girl so wide eyed and wild.
How you have grown and you did it alone
Yet inside you're still a child.
Sweet Street Rose how the time sure flows
Like rain from a fierce hurricane.
I've watched you bend like a flower in the wind
But you bounce back again.

When I was younger how I wanted to go
By way of Texas into Mexico.
Then to Oaxaca that's the way the wind blows
And find me a Spanish rose.

Today I'm younger and I don't know how.
But that's okay I'm alive right now
In the cold city fighting off the snows
Searching out Sweet Street Rose.
Sweet Street Rose does anyone know
The silence deep in your soul
Or feel the pain from the thorn in your name
Yet you shine as if gold.

For, Eileen and every woman who feels the changing of the seasons within her.

Human Seasons

Her eyes have searched and found the light of this life
Her spirit knows and soars to higher heights
The sun is love and on the other side
The moon hangs full in gemini
Human Seasons touch her tonight

She's a lady of the lakes and rivers
The crescent moon shines deep within her
A burning comet in the sky
Stardust in her soulful eyes

She feels nature giving birth through the air
The wind blowing through her soft rich hair
Whose voice was that she just heard
"Love is all the only word"
As seasons change with flying birds
Human seasons touch her tonight

TIME ON HAND

Time can't be praised and it can't be insulted
It can't be controlled or held onto by lies
It can't be slandered it can't be consulted
It can't be detained like a burgeoning sigh
You can test it--maybe it can be bent though
It can't be captured yet it's bound to be spent
Yes, it sure can be spent

Time can't be purchased and it cannot be owned
It can't be embarrassed but can be abused
You can lend it yet you can't get it on loan
Time will not take orders yet it can be used
So hard to find yet so easy to lose and
If you lose track you know it can't be brought back
No, it can't be brought back

Time goes on I can hear the hourglass drain
When time passes by it is forever gone
You run to a place take shelter from the rain
You can't hide from time in some broken down barn
You can't stop time no matter how hard you try
A fool just sits down and watches it fly by
And, watches it fly by

Time can't be held but it can be on your hands
You can't pick it up and you can't put it down
It's just like magic that we don't understand
Like the drifting and shifting of desert sands
Arranging and rearranging everything
Giving movement to water and land but yet
So little time on hand

TIME

Time has wings memories skip across the mind
Like flames dancing on a log
Where have the years gone
They pass like white lines on a highway
Fifty sixty seventy miles an hour
Fleeting floating colors gray clouds in your eye
A straight and endless highway a castle in the sky
Autumn in the country brisk wind blowing high
Winter in the city I don't want to die
A scent a smell a dying rose
A life to live one life and then it goes

Photo by Mark Epstein, *taken from the New York Times Magazine, 2/12/12 of the Hangman's Elm. No 28 Washington Square North, where I lived, is at the far right corner of the photo, only partially shown.*

Christmas Eve at Washing Square Park

I was only nine and have no recall of how mom and dad got it but they were interviewed for the Superintendent's job at 27-28 Washington Square North in Greenwich Village. It's the gray building on the Northeast corner of Washington Square North and MacDougal Street.

The following is from the book "Forgotten New York" by Kevin Walsh.

"3 MacDougal/27-28 Washington Square North is called The Richmond Hill Apartments, after a colonial estate in what is today the West Village. Built by Major Abraham Mortier in the 1770s and later used by General George Washington as a head-quarters, later owned by the 3rd. Vice President and killer of Alexander Hamilton, Aaron Burr. Matthew (Ferris Buehler) Broderick is a former resident.

The building that stands there now was built in 1898 by the Chisholm family as a "swing" building, constructed with odd layouts to the apartments, large rooms, high ceilings and long interior corridors; built to protect the land from being purchased up by industry. And, with the practical thought that the apartments could be converted into lofts, if the situation ever arose--it never arose. " Two weeks after their interview dad received a call from the landlord asking him when it would be possible to move in and take over their new job. Mom was excited, in the beginning, and felt that living in Greenwich Village would be good for all of us.

Because I liked the name so much I pleaded with mom to get Margie and I into Our Lady of Pompeii.

Continued...

After Mom had inquired she discovered there was no room at Pompeii so she got us into Saint Joseph's School of Greenwich Village. This Saint Joseph's was run by the Sisters of Charity not the Sisters of Notre Dame as was our Yorkville school.

"The Sloper residence in Henry James's novel, Washington Square (1881) was modeled on the home of James's grandmother who lived at 18 Washington Square--a few doors away from our new apartment. From his novel:

"It has (Washington Square) a kind of established repose which is not of frequent occurrence in other quarters of the long, shrill city; it has a riper, richer, more honourable than any of the other ramifications of the great longitudinal (5th Ave--author note) thoroughfare--the look of having had something of a social history." --Henry James WASHINGTON SQUARE

During the 1830's the Washington Square neighborhood became one of Manhattan's most desirable residential areas. As the new, aesthetically pleasing, Greek revival houses on the north side of Washington Square Park were being built the streets surrounding the square quickly became the place to live. The folk who established their elegant marble-trimmed brick homes alongside the north side of the park were nicknamed "the old Knickerbocker families" and referred to as New York's first families.

Sometime in 1951 my sister and I were told that we were moving to Greenwich Village. My sister was too young to be effected as much as I being older. I thought I'd die leaving Yorkville and all my friends behind. We lived on the street level in an apartment that had 10 rooms.

We had 4 windows that looked out onto MacDougal Street and two windows that opened onto the private and peaceful, MacDougal Alley where I played.

"Alexander McDougal (his father spelled it MacDougall with 2 L's and an A) was a commander in the Revolutionary War and an anti-British agitator in colonial days. A Scotsman, he arrived here from the Hebrides as a child, grew up here, piloted a ship for seven years, then settled down as a New York City merchant. He was the founder of the underground Sons of Liberty. He published a pamphlet condemning and accusing the Brits concerning their restrictions on trade and in 1770 they tossed him in jail. Later, he took over the post that Benedict Arnold vacated as commander of defenses of West Point and then represented New York in the Continental Congress. He became the first president of the Bank of New York and was a state senator when he died in 1786 at the age of 53.

The 19th-century stable houses in MacDougal Alley and Washington Mews (University Place to Fifth Avenue, between 8th Street and Waverly (spelled with one "e") Place--namesake of Sir Walter Scott's novel Waverley) were erected by the owners of the large row of houses on Washington Square North as their private carriage houses. By the early 1900's the area had become a slum. In 1892, sculptor, Frederick Triebel purchased #6 and converted it to a beautiful dwelling and a soothing place to do his work. Soon a slew of known artists began to buy up the stables and turn them into homes and places for work. Among these were: Gertrude Vanderbilt Whitney, Guy Pene du Bois, Jo Davidson, Ernest Lawson, James Fraser, Daniel Chester French, Henry Bush-Brown and Philip Martiny. Eventually people began to refer to McDougal Alley as 'Art Alley de Luxe'.

In McDougal Alley there was usually an older boy about 14 or so who watched out for his little brother, maybe two or three years old, I was nine. The older boy was David Carradine and the little guy, I think, was Keith. Sons of the much admired, Shakespearian actor, John, who also had many film roles in his active career. Mr. Carradine was tall and lanky and for me, his voice was intensely hypnotic. However, he was quite the gentleman. He had to walk past our kitchen windows in McDougal Alley to get to his own house, one of the old, beautiful, stable houses. Mom was usually washing dishes or preparing food near that window. Mr. Carradine never failed to say hello in passing, sometimes stopping and chatting for a moment. Mom was thrilled each time he past.

"We were neighbors and David was very nice to me. He took me for a ride one day on his bike all around Washington Square Park hopping curbs and flying down Bleecker Street into La Guardia Place, down to Houston, up Sixth Avenue across 8th Street, down MacDougal St and back into the park. People jumping out of our way while he kept ahead of the dogs chasing us in the park; the ride was action packed and intoxicating for this nine-year-old. I liked David, he treated me like a little brother and I missed him after we moved away.

By the 1920's and 30's MacDougal Alley was considered the most sophisticated place to live in Manhattan and continued to be a haven for writers, actors and artists of every sort. When we lived there Eddie Condon, the Jazz musician lived upstairs. Washington Mews with its Belgian-block pavement, McDougal Alley with its gas lamps and both with their quaint, storybook houses, still offer the serene feeling of a simple life in a tiny village.

From 1789 through 1823 the site of Washington Square Park was the city's first potter's field and its trees, some say, were used as the public gallows. On execution days the hangings drew large crowds of merrymakers, curiosity seekers, tourists, local drunks, and kids all crowding into the area to get a glimpse of the action. Potter's field was closed in 1823, four years later the park was laid out and the first of Washington Square North's magnificent mansions were erected. The remains of over 10,000 people are still buried in Washington Square Park.

1951/'52--Above Whelan's Drugstore

I became a little street urchin, indignant, an angry rebel, missing my friends, my school and my neighborhood, barely speaking to my parents. Never getting into deep trouble but out until all hours of the night. Dashing into a tie store at 7th Avenue and Sheridan Square, in broad daylight, grabbing a handful of ties (I didn't even wear ties, yet) with a classmate and running out. A policeman chasing me around Sheridan Square as I ran into a hallway ringing all the bells to get inside the second door and running up the first flight of stairs before being collared by the cop and kicked smartly in the behind--3 times. Lifting trinkets from the 5 &10 cents store on 6th Avenue and 4th Street and running through the streets. My dad was working two jobs, the first one as a chauffeur from 1 pm until 8 pm. He would go straight to his second job as a night doorman (he would sleep there for three hours before his shift started) where he worked from midnight until 8 am. He would go home and sleep for another 3 hours then get up and do it all over again. While mom's mood fell deep into despair, she would sit alone in the kitchen and listen to the Country radio station play their heartbreaking songs. Mom was very depressed during our time in the Village and drank too much.

My sister and I wanted so much to help her but did not know how. She was a good mother but for our time in the village where, I now know, her soul was being tortured. I could pretty well come and go as I pleased as long as my sister was okay. Living in such a large apartment, mom, never knew where we were anyway. In the evenings while my father worked I'd roam through the Village. One night I had just left my house and I was looking in a bookstore window, near our building, on the southeast corner of MacDougal and 8th Street next to Shakespeare's Bar and Restaurant, admiring the dust jackets on the books. I've always been in awe of books. The thought of having pieces of each writer's mind captured in a small box that opens up for anyone to read staggered me. I could stand there for hours looking through the glass at all those wonders. My concentration was broken when I heard a deep baritone voice say, "Do you like books, kid?" I looked up and there was a big man with Kaki Marine pants tucked into spit-shined boots. He looked just like a Marine but there was something about him that told me he wasn't. He wore a brown bomber jacket over a white Tee-shirt but, I noticed, he had no dog tags. He wore an army-crew-cut hairdo, his nails sparkled from a recent manicure and he smelled of Vitalis hair tonic. He was as sharp and clean as a butcher's knife before its first cut. I looked at him warily, turned back to the store window and casually said, "Sometimes." "What do you mean sometimes? Either you do or you don't."

"I don't read much but someday when I'm older and have the time, I will. Right now I go to school and don't have much time for reading." I paused, looked up, then asked: Do you have a lot of books?"

"Probably the largest collection of books you've ever seen."

My interest began to peak. "Oh yeah?"

"Sure do. I have books about everything you could imagine."

"How many books, like hundreds?" The man laughed and then with a stern look he said, "Thousands." Amazed, I blurted out.

"WHAT!"

"Photography books, history books, mystery books, science fiction books, poetry, classics, plays, all kinds of fiction and non-fiction. Man, do I have books."

"And you read them all?"

"I've read many of them but the others are books I'd like to read some day. Whenever I come across one that I want to read I'll buy it so anytime I have a desire to read a certain book chances are I'll have it on my shelf." The tension I felt at first began to dissipate, I became more open and talkative.

"That's just what I want some day. To have all these books and read anyone of them anytime I feel like it."

"I live right across the street over there on 8th St." He pointed, "The windows above Whelan's Drugstore on the corner are mine." I nodded. "Well that's my place. Would you like to see my books?" I looked at him and thought if this guy wanted to hurt me he could. I squinted at him and said: "No funny stuff. My brother's an Army Air Force SERGEANT and is sitting right over there in Shakespeare's with his buddies.

He'll come out of there and kill you if you ever tried any-
thing funny with his little brother." We both looked into
Shakespeare's. There was one person sitting at the bar
talking to the bartender and there was a young couple at
a table in a corner. I looked up at him and said: "He must
have gone into our house, we live right there," I pointed,
he smiled and said: "My name is Robert what's yours?"

"Dennis."

"Come on Dennis. You'll be back in ten minutes. All you
have to do is look at my books, maybe have a sandwich
and hot chocolate then you're back on the street, okay?" I
nodded and followed him. We walked across the street
and entered the building that Robert lived in. Up one
flight of carpeted stairs and when he opened the door to
his apartment I stood astonished at the number of books
decorating the walls of Robert's living quarters. My host
went into his kitchen and began to make noise with some
pots and dishes while I explored the bookshelves.

"How about a bologna sandwich with the hot chocolate?"
"I like bologna." "Bologna it is. Mustard and white bread
okay with you?" "Sure is." In a few minutes Robert
entered the living room with the food and the hot choco-
late on a tray and placed it on the table. He smiled and
said, "Eat hearty, my friend, I'll be back in a flash." I dug
into the sandwich, I hadn't eaten since that morning, and
slugged down the hot chocolate as I slowly navigated the
entire room perusing all the books. I stuck half the sand-
wich in my pocket for later, placed my cup down on a
side table and pulled a book off a shelf.

"Robert!"

"What is it?"

"Have you read HUCKLEBERRY FINN?"

"Yes I have, have you?"

"It was the first book I ever read," and thought, the only book I've ever read. Then I heard Robert enter the room and I turned. He was wearing a silk Paisley robe and carried two tumblers, one in each hand and I nearly choked on my sandwich when I looked at him. He said, "What was that you just said?" Wide-eyed and shocked I gulped out the words, "I said..., it was the only book I've ever read."

"Why don't you sit down and relax and have a brandy with me and we'll talk about the sexy part when Huck was with his little horny girlfriend in the cave, you remember that scene don't you?" I dropped the book on the floor and grabbed the butter knife, with mustard on it, from the bologna plate. Brandishing my weapon I shouted: "If you come near me I swear I'll stick you." I had fire in my eyes but Robert just grinned. He stood between me and the door. He casually lighted a cigarette, blew smoke at the ceiling, took a long drink of his brandy and in a soft voice said, "Do you think you could stop me from screwing you if I really wanted to? Not on your life you little gutter rat." Robert took a step closer to me, let his robe fall open and I could see that his desire had grown and that, really, was disturbing--it scared the hell out of me. He moved forward, another step toward me and began to smile with unblinking, anxious eyes. I backed into a small table knocking it and its contents, an ashtray, a framed photograph of Robert with another man and a small plant onto the floor.

Then tumbling backwards I landed on top of everything. But I was on my feet, immediately, shouting, "You come near me and I'll cut that thing off." Robert walked over to the wall, reached up and pulled down one of two fencing foils which were hanging there and sarcastically bleated out his threat, "I, my little friend, am an epeeist. That is, in case you don't understand, is one who fences with an epee." He slashed the air several times making it whistle in pain. "And THIS" (holding it with his two hands one on the handle and the other at the tip and flexing it above his head while bending his knees in syncopation) "is an epee." Then, in one smooth motion, Robert picked a throw pillow off his couch, tossed it into the air and drove his epee through it before it had reached chest high. "If I so desired I could cut you to pieces before anyone could hear you scream."

That was it! I flew past him and was at the door trying to get it open it while keeping one eye on Robert. I fumbled with the lock and the doorknob as my knees began to fail me. My heart beat so loud I thought it was going to explode. I was getting dizzy and could barely stand on my feet as Robert leaped into a fencing stance and began moving closer with each sentence until his foil was touching my forehead.

"I see you and your little sister wandering the streets all the time. I know you have no brother in the bar. I know I could do whatever I want to you and nobody would care." With my back to the door he watched me groping with the doorknob behind me in frustration and fear.

"Turn the top lock to the left and the door knob to the right." Then just as I got the door open Robert shouted and stomped his foot simultaneously. "Go on, you little shit-head. Get the fuck out of here."

I bounded from the apartment and went tumbling, head over heels, down the long flight of thickly carpeted stairs, bounced up onto my feet and squirted out onto 8th Street and I didn't stop running until I was home in my bed. The simple thought of what Robert, the burly, fake-ex-marine could have done to me if he wanted had my skin shaking on my bones.

Notwithstanding, Robert, the evil creep over Whelan's Drug Store, for the rest of my life I would be drawn back downtown to Greenwich Village. For me the 'Village' was a torch singer, brazen, brassy, crystal-eyed and the Queen of Mystery. Her pull was stronger than gravity as she whispered her secrets and her addictive blue rhapsody into my ears caressing this heart in her sweet and sour hands.

Christmas Eve, 1951--"THE CHRISTMAS SONG"

10 p.m.: We dressed warm, my sister and I, and went out-side and were standing on top of our stoop staring straight out into the park. It had been snowing lightly for quite some time and the park was deserted. The paths and the grass areas had all merged into one wavy, white landscape and the trees wore coats of tightly wound cot-ton as the snow crystalized into delicate sparkling spider webs among the branches. Many buildings surrounding the park were twinkling with colored Christmas lights of greens reds and blues like a rainbow cumulus encircling the park. Gazing into the park's hushed beauty with the stars flickering above the crystal night a lone dog stood in the center of an open field, staring up at one branch in a big, old tree and not moving a muscle. We studied a bag lady, one whom we had seen many times and thought her completely insane, as she circumnavigated the park she had something to say to each tree she passed.

"Den?" Anticipating my sister's question, I said, "You wanna build a snowman?"

"Oh please, please, please? Can we? We could build it right next to that big tree--it looks so lonely. Pretty please?" No one will ever know we were out this late. Dad won't be back tonight and mom is sound asleep. Okay?" We could hear the Church bells of St. Joseph's over on Sixth Avenue, chiming in the distance. I took my sister by the hand, looked around us and said, "It looks nice out here tonight, doesn't it?" She said, "It's just like a picture on a Christmas card." I said: "Lets go." We crossed Washington Square West into our own little dream of Christmas Eve and the silent night. We built a snowman near a great big old elm. When we finished we ran over to a group of garbage cans, outside the park, to spruce him up and give him a bit of character. Margie found two pieces of half-burnt coal in an ashcan on McDougall Street and gave him eyes. I gave him a big smile with a old orange peel and a peach pit-nose Margie found a discarded polo shirt and turned it into a perfect muffler for his neck. While rummaging through the garbage I grubbed up an old red and white, two quart metal cooking pot that made an excellent hat and Margie squealed with delight. That pot was waiting to be found. Now we were finished. We stepped back and surveyed our work in wonderment. Margie asked: "What's his name?"

I stared at my, newly turned, six-year-old sister. Her eyes were bright and twinkling with excitement and anticipation. I was responsible for her and I would do anything to protect her or at least to keep her smiling. A bell clanged inside my chest and I wanted to say something grown-up but all that came out was: "You should name him, Marg, he's really yours."

"How about if we call him Gabriel after the Archangel?"

"What's with the Archangel stuff?"

"He's one of the tough ones that can protect people and fight the bad angels. Isn't he? That's what Mom says."

"I guess so. Mom knows her angels."

"Well maybe if we name him Gabriel we can ask him to protect mom when she drinks." Gazing into a face of pure sincerity I couldn't speak. I turned my head so she wouldn't see the tears beginning to sear my eyes. She stood there looking up at me waiting for an answer. When I had control I leant over, kissed her on the forehead, and: "Okay, he's Gabriel." We sat down on the soft snow between the big old elm tree and our dapper snowman, Gabriel, and stared into the park.

After a short time we went into our apartment and into our own rooms. I was under the covers listening to Mom's Country and Western Station coming from the kitchen. That Christmas Eve Mom's anger began to build until she grabbed hold of her ironing cord and showed up at the foot of my bed. I was up and running as she chased me through the 10 room apartment. I could hear my sister shouting from her room: "Stop it Mom! Leave him alone." She caught me one time across my shoulders before I was able to gather all my clothes and scramble out into the hallway. (This type of situation happened three times while we lived in the village and never again, after Mom got better. I don't know why but I know she was suffering and it hurt her more than, I think, it hurt me.) Trembling with anger and shame I clumsily dressed and went off into the night.

I began to run as the names of the streets flew past me: 4th Street, Bleecker, 3rd Street, Sullivan, La Guardia Thompson, Houston, 8th Street, Minetta Lane. I collapsed on the steps of St. Joseph Church at Washington St. and 6th Ave--not far from our apartment, I had been running in a circle. I looked up at the brooding red doors to the church where I was supposed to serve mass that coming Sunday. Right there and then I decided I would never serve another mass again, as long as I lived; because nothing was right, the entire world was all wrong. I sat there about ten minutes, stood up and began to walk up 6th Avenue cut across Greenwich to Seventh then down to Barrow where I met a quiet kid from my class. We walked awhile just talking. Back on Sixth Avenue outside the Women's House of Detention he began to look at his Mickey Mouse watch and then up at the jail. It was exactly midnight, Christmas Eve and church bells were exploding all over the city. My friend was jumpy and paced back and forth glancing at his watch as the snow whispered down around us. Tommy stepped off the curb and into Sixth Avenue, shaded his eyes from the glare of bright lights while staring up at the bulky, oppressive orange brick, Art Deco building. I stood there wondering. Then, I heard, "Tommy! Tommy, are you there?"

"I'm here Ma!"

"Merry Christmas Honey. I love you." Tommy put his two hands to his mouth and made a tunnel with them giving his words wings to fly as he shouted back to his mother: "Merry Christmas, Ma. I love you too."

"Are you taking care of your brother? Don't forget you've got to take care of your brother. He needs you. Promise me honey?"

"I promise, Ma."

"And go right home. Okay?"

"Don't worry Ma. I'm not a baby."

Tommy put his head down, started to walk away. I had my head turned and was looking back and up at the top floor windows in the jail. When I searched for Tommy I spotted him halfway to 11th Street and I heard him call to me, "Let's walk up to 42nd Street and see what people do on Christmas Eve" I nodded and ran across West 10th Street to catch up with him. We walked about fifteen yards together then we heard: "Tommy. Be careful!" We looked at one another, I felt uncomfortable. Tommy bent his head low for a moment then looked back at me. We began to walk, after advancing a few more yards I felt Tommy's arm go around my shoulders. We proceeded to walk all the way up to 42nd. Street, with our arms around each other's shoulders. The previous month I saw two old men playing chess in Washington park. I walked over and planted myself down beside the older man. About ten minutes had passed and neither of the players had uttered a sound. I thought they had fallen asleep. Suddenly, the one next to me began to cough and gag as his entire body joined in and began to shake and shiver until he spat up a marble thing that bounced once off the concrete walk before disappearing into the grass. He reached into the band of his old, brown pea-cap and pulled out a half smoked Dinobli cigar. He fumbled in the pocket of his plaid-flannel shirt, came out with a wooden matchstick, struck it with the nail of his right thumb, lighted his stinker, took a lung full of smoke, let it drift out of his nostrils as he closed his eyes and to no one in particular said: Yep, my great-grandaddy was one of the

last men to be hanged from that beastly, old Hanging Elm back in 1823....., or was it 1824?" He said scratching his stubble, "Anywise," he went on, "they hanged nineteen other men that same day while half the citizens of this city filled the park and picnicked with all sorts of festivities during them hangings. They was all drinking and dancing around, they was jumping and cheering every time another one of them criminals dropped." He opened his eyes and with a long, knobby finger he pointed at the big tree in front of our building and said, "Right there near the corner of McDougal and Washington Square North. The Hanging Elm." He paused for a moment before resuming his story... "I've heard tell that Frenchy feller, what's his name now, oh yes, the Marquis de Lafayette was here for them hangings and watched the whole thing. Don't know if that's true or not. Some say yea and some say nay. My great-grandaddy, he was a thief and a murderer and most certainly deserved hanging. He killed a man for three measly dollars. Man who was sleeping on one of these benches right here in this park. An hour after the man's body was discovered they found my grandaddy sitting in a saloon over on Bleecker Street working on what was left of that man's three dollars; still had the man's wallet on him. I guess you could say he was more than a few feet short of a mile." He blustered out a laugh, spit out another marble, turned his head, pointed his watery, ice-blue-eyes down at me and said: "Hear me now boy?" I nodded and a throaty "Yes" came from my mouth. The old man leaned over and went nose-to-nose with me. His whisper hit like a veil of cigar smoke, wine and garlic. He said, "Did you know that that old 'Hanging Elm' is the oldest living thing in New York City, boy? Just like me, I'm the oldest living human in Greenwich Village what moves." Then his opponent said:"Oh, leave the kid alone, why don't cha Pete?"

"I'm trying to teach him something." He became serious again. "I know you, boy, I see you taking your sister to school in the mornings, you live in that big old gray house, near the old elm. Some say, too many men were hanged from it's branches and, if you put your ear up against her, ya can hear the last breath of each man as he swung to and fro, to and fro." He leaned in to me again and in a stage whisper, said: "The old gravedigger lived right over there on the south side of Thompson Street in a little old shack. Rent free, I'll have you."

When I came home that Christmas Day morning, after walking the night away with Tommy, I was thinking of the things the old chess player had said to me. The light was swallowing the dark with a hugh morning yawn and it was contagious. I knew Mom would be sound asleep. I looked for Gabriel by the elm and there wasn't a trace of him, as if he never existed. I thought I might have imagined the entire time I spent building the snowman with Margie. I looked up at the oldest living thing in New York City and I stared. I would have bet my life, that tree was staring back at me.

I sat down on the top step of my stoop watching the early rambunctious dogs take their owners out for runs through the snow in the park. I thought about my sister and our time last night just before we went back into our apartment when she leant her head against my arm and said: "I'll always remember this Christmas, Den. Will you remember it when we get old?" I slid my arm around my sister's back and said: "I'll never forget it, Marg."

She snuggled closer and we sat that way in the quiet night. The air was clean, fresh and snappy and it looked like a million stars were casting their light down on,

Washington Square Park. Spotlighting a brother and sister soaking it all up on Christmas Eve. We heard an argument over on 8th Street where it meets McDougal Street. A party was happening on a floor above in the building we lived in, every so often a car horn went off over on Sixth Avenue and close by Nat King Cole's voice came from an open window: "Chestnuts roasting by an open fire, Jack Frost nipping at your nose."

As Mr. Cole's song ended, somewhere off in the distance, we heard a gospel group, in the street, begin to sing, loud and clear: "Silent Night, Holy Night"

No! I will never forget.

Full Moon at Castle Lake

It was a cool, clear, sweet smelling city night. The Sun marched through Libra, the Moon was full in Aries and activity flourished everywhere. Chuck felt the snapping of electricity in the air like a kid in the grip of puppy love. Not only could he hear and see the night but he felt it on his skin and he felt it rushing through his veins. He could taste it in his mouth and in his soul. The voice of the full Moon spoke to him loud and clear, giving him a riddle and telling him this was no ordinary night.

MOONSHINE

by waters where I lie there is a sterling studded sky
a castle up on high
diamond webbing weaves the scene
of purple blue and green
my blankets the dark I see it's so deep
it starts at a star and ends at my feet
that man in a dream we are the same
he only nods when you ask his name
come with me my friend take this road to the end
follow a fountain to the foot of a mountain
where a child plays naked with bows in her hair
the touch of silk seems to come from my dreams
while the crack of a fire sends heat through the air
roses are real love is a meal for people
with velvet tongues
the heavens it seems have split at the seams
and put Moonshine deep in my lungs

It was nearing midnight on a Saturday, a beautiful, late September evening, in Nineteen Sixty-Nine. Chuck was four hours into his usual 4 day 13 hour taxi shift. After six months of continuous growth he was not too proud of his sparse mustache. But his hair was beginning to brush his shoulders and he was proud of that. Whenever possible, Chuck would roll up and down the streets of Greenwich Village looking for fares in his big Checker taxi. For anyone seeking to be overwhelmed by the Spirit of the Sixties, New York's East Village was the place to be. During the late Sixties and early Seventies, Chuck drove his cab around New York City and picked up many Rock superstars who played at the Fillmore East during those days. He loved driving his taxi and was not surprised to find himself completely lost in the merry-go-round song of the city's pounding pulse. With Bob Dylan screeching out from his cassette player, Chuck enjoyed the sights as he drove around. The streets teemed with people. Flower children gave away flowers, tourists posed for pictures with hippies and hobos wore beads and sang songs. Everywhere he went music filled the air while the city's brew bubbled away. He joined a policeman dancing with five laughing ladies from Wisconsin while a group of Hell's Angels stood around them applauding. This night was definitely different than any other night. Since it was so lovely people wanted to be out walking and that caused business to drop off some. Of course Chuck did not care or even have a mind for business this night.

Pulling his cab over at 73rd. Street and 3rd Avenue Chuck went into his favorite coffee shop to say hello to his friend, Nick, who was proud to serve the worst coffee anywhere on Third Avenue. They chatted for a spell and then Chuck said: "Will I get a fresh cup of coffee in the morning, Nick?"

"You get what you get every Sunday morning, Chuukee."

Getting off his stool, dropping a dollar on the counter, Chuck smiled as he picked up his dinner. Already knowing Nick's response he headed for the door as he asked: "And what's that my friend?"

"You get what's left, we never make fresh coffee here, it's against the law. Ha, ha, ha! See you in the morning, Chuukee."

Chuck got back into his chariot with his coffee and a jelly donut to kill the taste of the coffee. He kept returning to the same shop because he got a kick out of Nick. As he dined, he watched two young men in their twenties standing about thirty feet in front of his cab. They looked like they were waiting for a taxi but were in deep conversation. Several empty cabs whizzed by and they paid no attention to them, so, Chuck lost interest. Although he could not help notice they were both wearing three piece tweed suits and had long flowing beards. If that weren't enough to get his scrutiny they also wore wire rim glasses and were puffing on two enormous white pipes. As Chuck finished his coffee the two characters walked straight towards him. The shorter one opened the back door and they both climbed in. When Chuck turned and asked: "Where to?" he thought he was facing the Smith Brothers who had just escaped from the front of a cough drop box. The shorter one with the shorter beard began directing Chuck and calling him by his name. Chuck figured he must have seen his license with his name on it, some people will do that. Then the little one introduced himself as, Jack and his friend as, John, and said: "Go down Fifth Avenue to Washington Square Park, lets just drive around the village for awhile. If that's all right with you, Chuck?" As Jack continued to talk, Chuck noticed they both wore bow ties. Aside from being the shorter, one, the 'talker' Jack was slim and frail, had shifty eyes and made Chuck slightly uncomfortable. Jack kept talking, "Then we'll go around the park and east on 8th Street." If Jack was five-foot-five, John was six-foot-two and wiry. John's bow tie was a paisley print which seemed to go with his subdued personality, compared to his chatty friend, Jack, with the bright red bow tie.

The first time, Chuck stopped for a light he turned and took a long look at his two passengers. John sat smiling, puffing away on his large pyramid-shaped pipe. Jack suddenly shoved his own pipe in front of Chuck's face while pointing out directions. The bowl of his pipe had a hand carved devil with wings sitting on the front of it. The likeness was so real it startled Chuck as he gasped for air and jerked his head back. In a soft but deep rolling voice, John told him they were given the pipes by a man from the ancient, sunken continent of Lemuria, which was called, The Land of MU, and they were made from the wood of magical trees.

They explained to Chuck that Jack was having marital problems after only two years of marriage. With a furtive look in his eyes, Jack said: "I believe my wife is having an affair and I am very angry and, at the least, intend to leave her."

John was doing his utmost to convince Jack to try and work things out. Then with a smile John said: "Jack should not be so rapid in his conclusions, right Chuck?" Nodding, Chuck watched the meter tick away as he barreled all around the city while listening to his strange passengers.Three to four hours passed before, Chuck began to feel like he was inside of a cartoon. What were these guys smoking in their wooden pipes made from magical trees in the land of MU? Who was the guy who gifted them with these pipes? Chuck told them he was beginning to feel disoriented and was worried about his driving. John, observing Chuck's uneasiness remarked: "Some food would do us all well. Lets stop by the deli at 4th Street and 6th Ave." Chuck pulled over, Jack jumped out and in a flash returned with sandwiches and assorted soft drinks. Then they drove up 6th Avenue and entered Central Park. They parked in the parking lot near the confection stand by Rowboat Lake, shut the cab down and walked to Castle Lake, all the while eating and discussing marriage.

There, high above the lake, looking as though it had been carved out of the rocks, stood Belvedere Castle. It seemed all the stars in the Universe were on this side of the hemisphere that night. The immensity of the full Moon, the castle hanging above the lake and all this beauty reflecting back off the water. As he soaked it all in, he thought: magic in its purest form. Then Jack handed Chuck his pipe while he stretched out and studied the sky. After a moment Jack sat up with a twisted smile on his face and pointed at Chuck and asked: "Do you know the riddle?" Chuck was stunned by a powerful feeling of melancholia that swept over him. Through the years Castle Lake had always been a special place he found comforting yet unsettling. Quite often he would find himself under one of the trees that border the banks of the lake, arrested by the beauty of the entire scene. Even as a young boy after playing baseball in the park, he and some of his friends would come here to rest before returning home. Whenever he seemed to have an unsolvable problem, this is where he would come to work things out. Now here he was with these two bizarre gents beneath a full moon, and for some reason he felt as though he were losing control, as if he were on some sort of drug. The one thing Chuck never did was drugs. He loved life and felt he could get as high as anyone just by looking at a flower, seeing a child play, or watching the rising and setting of the Sun.

While these thoughts ran through Chuck's mind he felt a terrible pain in his left thumb. He looked down at his hand which held Jack's pipe and the devil on the bowl had turned its head and was biting his thumb. Screaming in pain and fright the pipe flew into the air.

On making contact with the ground the pipe exploded in a maze of purple and blue smoke. When the cloud cleared there were about twenty people spread out on 3 blankets. There was food, wine and all the makings for a picnic including two guys playing guitars, a girl playing a harmonica and a little girl running around with ribbons in her hair.

John was playing one of the guitars. He wore dungarees, sandals, a flowered shirt and beads circled his neck. Jack was on another blanket with a tall, beautiful black girl who had, what looked to be, the largest Afro in the world. They were into some serious necking, while John led everyone in singing LUCY IN THE SKY WITH DIA-MONDS. As Chuck struggled to comprehend what was real and what was not, he felt a hand begin to rub his calf as he stood up and stared at all the activity. The hand slowly inched its way up his leg. He tried to see who was at the end of the hand but an unseen force prevented him from looking down.

As it tugged at his pants he fell to his knees and was able to see it, finally. The hand in its movement, so slow and

sexy, so feminine and delicate. Chuck began to breathe heavily. Mustering every bit of strength he could draw from within himself he managed to turn his head slightly. Just enough to see the thin wrist and slim arm that belonged with the hand. Now it pulled him closer. So sensual was the hand when he looked that his heart began to pound uncontrollably. There were rings on four fingers some fingers wore two rings. The hand slid up his arm, over his shoulder and behind his neck. At last, turning, he found himself looking into the most beautiful eyes he had ever seen surrounded by the face of an angel. She was the girl of his most wildest fantasies and he knew her face well. Chuck tried desperately to gain control over what was happening but to no avail. He was lost in the powerful whirlwind of her being.

Then she pulled him down on top of her, instantly her breath was all around his mouth. He tasted her in every cell of his body. She slid her hands under his shirt, rubbed his bare back with them and squeezed him tightly against her warmth. He was on the edge of insanity. All he could feel was her, all he could see were explosions. He wanted to scream and tell her he loved her. Now she was kissing him down along his neck. He pulled back taking her head in his hands and looked into her eyes. Two black whirlpools began to carry him away but why did he feel as if he had come home? Why did he feel he knew this black-eyed beauty yet knew her not? and why did it all feel so comfortable? There was one thing Chuck did know and that was, wherever she was going, he was going. In a wink, Chuck was standing by the edge of the lake. Except for the fat moon and Belvedere Castle staring down at him--he was all alone. All he could think was:

WHERE IS SHE?

As he was winding his way back to his taxi his thoughts were of Jack and John. He wondered how they could have slipped him LSD without him knowing. Then again the girl with the whirlpool eyes was very real. He reached his taxi, slid onto the driver's seat and rested his head on the steering wheel. Suddenly he was hit on the side of his head by a large cloud of smoke. Nearly jumping out of his skin he almost broke his neck as he spun around. There they were in the back seat with their three piece suits and magical pipes. John intoned: "Jack would like you to meet his wife. He feels it is vital if he is to salvage his marriage. Since you, Chuck, have been married and divorced we feel that you have much to offer in experience and knowledge. You have listened to us discuss Jack's problem openly and have offered some excellent advise."

Chuck was lost and could not remember any of this only that Jack and his wife were having problems. He also knew that he was in no condition to give advise on anything, especially something as important as marriage. Chuck also wondered how they knew he had been married and divorced because he never spoke of it to anyone. He was about to tell them that they were both crazy as he put the key in the ignition to start the motor. As he did the whole scene changed and he found himself walking up a second flight of stairs in a brownstone somewhere in the West Eighties. As he arrived at the top floor apartment the door was wide open and he knew he had to go in. Smoke and music poured from the room and it was New Year's Eve, Nineteen Twenty-Eight. Inside the apartment all the men were wearing tuxedos and some of the women wore flapper outfits. The dancing was frenzied as people danced and drank bathtub gin. A few men had taken their jackets off and several of them wore shoulder holsters with guns. Jack was sitting on a couch and was clean shaven. His hair was parted down the middle and slicked back like most of the other men, only in a slightly different variation. Then Chuck saw the black girl from the park was sitting next to Jack. She wore short hair in an ironed down fashion. Chuck perused the scene carefully and perceived all the people at the party were the same ones who were at the park by the lake. Bessie Smith began to moan from the Victrola about Careless Love. Everyone began to move in slow motion, Chuck looked at his watch and it was one-twenty-two a.m. When he looked up again he saw John's face filling his view. Big John looked cold blooded and indifferent with his pencil line mustache. Like a record moving at slow speed John began to resonate and point across the room saying: "This is Lilith, Jack's wife." Her head was lowered as she cranked up the Victrola to start "Careless Love Blues" all over again. When she heard her name spoken by John, she lifted her head, looked across the room into Chuck's eyes. *My God, it's her!* Chuck thought. Her hair was curly and she wore a headband, she was perfect and absolutely beautiful. Chuck knew every inch of her: her lips, her neck, her breasts, the way she stood, the angle of her head and the hypnotic stare from the depths of her eyes.

Yes, those eyes made Chuck forget everything, he saw nothing but Lilith. He had the sensation of falling into a bottomless abyss as his stomach climbed up into his mouth. He started towards her, slow-footed and thought he would never reach her across the twenty-foot room. She was smiling, waiting for him. Her arms reached out as he heard his name being called out behind him. He turned and the first thing he saw was his reflection in a large mirror above the couch where Jack was sitting. Look at me! he mumbled, shiny hair and tuxedo I look like George Raft. For the first time Chuck felt the weight of

his own gun beneath his jacket. Out of the corner of his
eye he spotted a little girl in the next room with pig-tails
and two little red bows at their ends. Instantly he wanted
to pick her up. This little girl, he knew, was his and
Lilith's! Now he remembered their dark secret. He and
Lilith are deeply in love and no one knows this is their
child, they believe she is Jack's little girl. Suddenly Jack is
furious about something. He is trying to get up from the
couch but the black girl keeps pulling him back down
telling him:

"No, Jack. No!" Jack pulls his gun out and slaps the girl
across the face with it. She falls back onto the couch
unconscious. Jack turned his face to Chuck and screamed:

"CHARLIE!" Then the gun exploded in a blast of fire and
Chuck felt the heat from the discharge hit him in the face.
He could see the bullet coming in slow motion as it
passed just below his right ear. Frantically he spun
around to see it rip through Lilith's shoulder and crash
into the wall behind her. Chuck rushed toward Lilith
reaching out to her as Jack screamed a second time:

"CHAAARRRLIEEE!" Another loud explosion and
Chuck thought someone had hit him with a baseball bat
across his back as he flew forward from the force of the
bullet. Falling into Lilith's arms as she was sliding down
the wall, he saw the bullet come out of his own chest and
pass into Lilith's throat. All became silent and black as the
two crumbled to the floor in a tangled heap.

Somewhere off in the distance, through a foggy haze, he
heard his name being called. John was speaking: "I hope
he'll be alright." He must have inhaled too much of the
opium we were smoking and got himself a contact high."

Chuck was sitting with his back against a tree staring out over Castle Lake when he heard Jack say: "Snap out of it Chuck!" John and Jack took Chuck under each of his arms and lifted him to his feet. The first thing Chuck saw was the daylight. It was very early morning and the birds were trying to wake up the world. While they helped Chuck back to the taxi John said: "Why did you run away?" Last night when you were about to drive us to Jack's to meet his wife you suddenly bounded from the cab and ran off into the night."

John explained how he and Jack had searched for him for hours only to find him a few minutes ago sitting under that tree. Then Jack responded: "It is time for us to go now, Charlie." They both thanked him for the evening and paid him handsomely. Chuck stood and watched them as they disappeared into the park. Chuck wondered if he had heard correctly. Did Jack call him, Charlie?

Now 7:00 a.m. on a Sunday morning in New York City, at times, can be as quiet as any small town in the country. The difference is you might not find a coffee shop with the assortment of weirdos like you'd find at Nick's all night diner. Chuck was very hungry after his night with the Smith Brothers and he needed someone from this planet to speak to before he went insane. When he walked in Nick grinned at him, exposing two upper gold teeth and said: "Why you drive all night with no license? You leave it here when you stop for dinner."

Nick dropped the license on the counter next to the stale donut and the bad coffee. Chuck stared at the license and mumbled: "How the hell did those guys know my name if my license wasn't in the cab?" Answering his own question he looked at Nick and said:"Because none of this ever happened." Chuck laid money on the counter, still mumbling to himself: "That's right. Those guys do not exist." Then Nick, gesticulating wildly, quickly added: "When I see your license on the counter I run out to catch you but you were already driving away with those guys with the beards."

Chuck was freezing and sweating at the same time as he sped around Manhattan Island. Down the East River Drive and up the Westside Highway, not searching for passengers but answers to questions that unhinged and terrorized him.

The next thing Chuck knew he was sitting under his favorite tree gawking at Castle Lake, trying to make sense out of the past 8 hours. Slowly an overwhelming sadness came over him. A tear wended its way down his cheek Anger began to build inside of him and he began to sweat profusely. He became enraged as turbulence rose up from his stomach. He clenched his left hand and hit the soft ground with it and a severe pain shot straight up his arm. He looked down in irritation at a swollen aching thumb which was turning black and blue and showing signs of an infection setting in. In the center of his nail he could see what looked like two little teeth marks.

A wave of understanding washed through his consciousness and he knew that Lilith and Charlie were somewhere under Castle Lake.

Dennis John Ferado
TAXI DRIVER

Dennis John Ferado